# DAY BY DAY

### THRIVING AFTER SEXUAL ABUSE AND TRAUMA

### JANET FEIL

## PRAISE FOR DAY BY DAY

Janet Feil helps those who have been fractured by sexual abuse to walk through a series of practical and personal steps toward wholeness. Spiritual but not overly spiritualized, Janet shares from the perspective of one who was, but is no longer broken, giving hope to anyone who has had their life shattered by sexual abuse that they can, timber by timber, restore the wholeness to life.

*Michael Gantt*
  *Pastor, Missionary, Author*
  *Michael Gantt Ministries*

Janet Feil contributes a most valuable discussion of a most devastating subject – abuse, especially sexual abuse, hidden in the tortured hearts, minds, and emotions of untold numbers of silent sufferers. She offers a safe, compelling path toward freedom.

*Dr. David J. Niquette*
  *Pastor, Fort Collins CO*

Janet Feil's *Day by Day* is a profoundly honest book. Her forty days of readings are based on personal, painful experience that through decision, faith, and persistence has entered genuine, joyful healing. You will find in these pages someone who understands you and gives you credible hope.
  *Peter Lundell*
  *D.Miss., pastor, writer, and teacher*

Janet Feil is a brave and beautiful woman who has walked her own journey of recovery with tenderness and integrity. In this book she offers with great generosity both wisdom and encouragement, rooted in her own experiences, for other survivors of sexual abuse. The book is an inspiring resource for those curious about their own stories and how to slowly take steps forward towards greater spiritual and emotional health.

Tracy Johnson
    www.redtentliving.com

Your book is bringing freedom to THIS survivor and has revealed more important details of some of my repressed abuse memories which have surfaced. I was able to receive truth and peace and encouragement from God. I am freer today than I was at the beginning of this week! I know you were addressing some very poignant topics that resonated with my traumas! I admire how you are taking courageous steps to share your story for God's glory. It has already helped me heal! Thank you for that gift.

~*An Overcomer*

DAY BY DAY is an independent work
Copyright 2018 by Janet Feil
All Right Reserved. This publication may not be reproduced, stored in a retrieval system, or transmitted in whole or in part, in any form or by any means, electronic, mechanical, photocopying, recording, or otherwise without the prior written permission of Janet Feil.

Scripture taken from the New King James Version® (NKJV). Copyright © 1982 by Thomas Nelson. Used by permission. All rights reserved.

Scriptures marked NIV are taken from the NEW INTERNATIONAL VERSION (NIV): Scripture taken from THE HOLY BIBLE, NEW INTERNATIONAL VERSION ®. Copyright© 1973, 1978, 1984, 2011 by Biblica, Inc.™. Used by permission of Zondervan.

Scriptures marked MSG are taken from *THE MESSAGE*, copyright © 1993, 1994, 1995, 1996, 2000, 2001, 2002 by Eugene H. Peterson. Used by permission of NavPress. All rights reserved.

Scripture quotations marked (NLT) are taken from the Holy Bible, New Living Translation, copyright © 1996. Used by permission of Tyndale House Publishers, Inc. Wheaton Illinois 60189. All rights reserved.

Scriptures marked NSECB are taken from the NEW STRONG'S EXHAUSTIVE CONCORDANCE OF THE BIBLE: All Greek and Hebrew words are italicized. They are taken from The NEW STRONG'S EXHAUSTIVE CONCORDANCE OF THE BIBLE, James Strong, 1990 copyright© by Thomas Nelson Publishers.

# CONTENTS

| | |
|---|---|
| *Introduction* | ix |
| *My Story* | xvii |

| | |
|---|---|
| Day 1: God Loves You | 1 |
| Day 2: Know Jesus | 5 |
| Day 3: Discover Yourself | 9 |
| Day 4: Bible Reading | 15 |
| Day 5: Identify the Words | 21 |
| Day 6: Name It | 25 |
| Day 7: Finding Your Voice | 31 |
| Day 8: A Safe Place | 35 |
| Day 9: Call On Me | 41 |
| Day 10: My Confidence Is in Christ | 47 |
| Day 11: Every Day Is a New Day | 51 |
| Day 12: Life is Messy | 55 |
| Day 13: It is Not Your Fault | 59 |
| Day 14: God Reveals One Memory at a Time | 65 |
| Day 15: How God Sees Me | 71 |
| Day 16: Our Thoughts Affect Our Actions | 75 |
| Day 17: Don't Hurry, Take Time to Think | 81 |
| Day 18: Listening Well and Asking Good Questions | 87 |
| Day 19: First Thoughts of the Day | 93 |
| Day 20: Help—I Don't Like Myself | 97 |
| Day 21: Allowing Time to Heal | 103 |
| Day 22: How to Care for Yourself | 109 |
| Day 23: Boundaries | 113 |
| Day 24: Trust | 119 |
| Day 25: Kindness | 123 |
| Day 26: Stand Firm Against the Enemy | 129 |
| Day 27: Laugh Again | 133 |
| Day 28: Ask God How to Love | 137 |
| Day 29: Resting in God | 143 |

| | |
|---|---|
| Day 30: Practice, Practice, Practice | 147 |
| Day 31: Forgiveness | 151 |
| Day 32: The Difference Between Being a Victim and a Survivor | 157 |
| Day 33: We Are Overcomers | 163 |
| Day 34: Growing in Grace | 169 |
| Day 35: Whose Story Have You Heard? | 173 |
| Day 36: How to Respond to Another Person's Story | 177 |
| Day 37: Write Your Story | 181 |
| Day 38: There Will Be Opposition | 187 |
| Day 39: Who Knows? | 191 |
| Day 40: Say "Yes" to God | 197 |
| *Afterword* | 201 |
| *About the Author* | 205 |
| *Acknowledgments* | 207 |
| *Recommended Book List* | 211 |
| *Journey Groups* | 213 |
| *Books Mentioned* | 215 |
| *Feeling Words Chart: Positive* | 217 |
| *Feeling Words Chart: Negative* | 223 |
| *Notes* | 229 |

*Dedicated to:*
*Men and women who have been sexually abused as children.*

# INTRODUCTION

Sexual abuse is a silent epidemic. It is found in every country, race, and on every economic level. It can involve anyone from presidents to leaders, pastors to church members, individuals in business and industry, high level and low level leaders, people in this country and worldwide. It cripples every person affected. In some cases, sexual abuse is a generational sin passed from one generation to the next. The statistics are that one out of every 4 women and one out of 6 men are victims of sexual abuse.

The effects of abuse are severe, whether it occurs one time or many. The pain, lies, damage to our dignity, instability, fears, shame, loss of integrity, inability to think clearly, and loss of self-esteem are all enormous things to overcome.

God meant for sex to be a beautiful intimacy between a husband and wife. Satan took what God designed for our wellbeing and did everything he could to destroy it. From the beginning of time people have been wounded and enslaved by every imaginable method of sexual harm to destroy the beauty God created in the hearts of human beings.

People who are wounded have lost their voice and cannot

speak out against the predators, abusers, johns, men in high places, and law enforcement personnel because of threats, death, bribes, or whatever else it takes to keep them silenced.

Victims lose both the ability to process clearly and the vocabulary to speak out against manipulative abusers who twist, lie, accuse or blame them. When they do, who will believe them? Predators are manipulative, are smooth talkers, and are very believable. Who will speak against a good guy, or a man of high social standing? Predators and abusers are well-versed in lying and convincing others they are not to blame; they can buy people off.

In families, children have been burned, have had a gun held to their head, been whipped, beaten, denied food, locked in closet, tied to beds, and other abuses that are difficult to imagine. They are threatened in order to keep them silent.

Children who are abused sometimes do not remember their trauma because of the early age at which they were abused. Others cannot remember a time they were not abused, not knowing another way of life—one of safety, security, dignity, stability, not being abandoned or neglected.

Abuse damages the brain. Research reveals holes in the brains of abused persons due to poisonous chemicals that flow through the brain of anyone who is traumatized. Only when the truth is revealed and thought patterns change and good chemicals flow through the brain, can the holes heal and give health back to the victim.

Victims become survivors after they face the truth about the trauma they have endured, speak the words of harm done to them, experience sorrow and sadness, and grieve their losses. This is the work of the survivor to overcome. It is hard work and may take months to heal with the help of a counselor. Survivors need a safe place with safe people, where they can learn to trust, love, think new thoughts, and be encouraged and valued by people who love and care for them.

The public does not know how damaging sexual abuse is. Rape is included in sexual abuse. The victim feels traumatized, never able to overcome unless they speak up and speak out. Every abused person has a different story; no two stories are alike. The harm done is so much greater than can be imagined. People who haven't been abused cannot grasp the depths of the trauma, pain, and damage. They say it is "water under the bridge; get over it." This indifference can isolate and shut down the victim even more. It brings pain upon pain.

**The definition of the problem:**

Sexual abuse involves any contact or interaction whereby a vulnerable person (often a child or adolescent) is used for the sexual stimulation of an older, stronger, or more influential person. Sexual abuse is much broader than forced, unforced, or stimulated intercourse. It includes touching, rubbing, or patting that is meant to arouse sexual pleasure in the offender. It may also involve visual, verbal, or psychological interaction where there is no physical contact.

Visual sexual abuse may involve exposing a victim to pornography or to any other sexually provocative scene (including exposure to showering, intercourse, or various stages of undress).

Verbal sexual abuse involves an attempt to seduce or shame a child by use of sexual or suggestive words.

Psychological sexual abuse includes interactions where a child is regularly used to play the role of an adult spouse, confidant, or counselor. For example, a mother who tells her 12-year-old son her sexual frustrations with his father and shares her deep thoughts and feelings with him in a way that invites him to a level of adult intimacy, has violated the young man's sexual identity.* *When Trust is Lost*, Dan Allender.

If you have been abused or know someone who has been abused, or is being abused, then listen to them, love them, and care for them. Get help. Do not force them to tell you anything; give them time. They do not know if it is safe to tell you, if you can be trusted, whether you will gossip or if you can keep a confidence.

Sexual abuse is a crime against society. Do not turn your face away when you see someone being abused by another. If you are not able to stand up against the abuser, find someone who can. Do not allow the victim to be alone with the abuser.

It is time sexual abusers pay for their crimes. Stand up; speak out. Be bold and educate whomever you need to educate in order to release victims from their abusers. I have heard so many who have been abused say that no one spoke up for them, no one rescued them, no one asked questions, and no one seemed to care.

My prayer is that you will be intentional in your observation of those around you. Love them and care for the hurting. Educate yourself, ask questions, be available, and support those who are doing the work of helping sexually abused people. It takes time, dedication, energy, prayer, and resources to minister to those who have a wounded heart.

This book is meant to be read again and again. Feel free to underline and write in the margins to help in your healing process.

## My Journey

As I looked back over the twelve years since I had been set free on my journey of healing, I felt God leading me to tell my story of how I learned to continue living and how to thrive in the process of staying mentally and emotionally healthy after recognizing the truth of my story.

I hear many people say, "Oh, I dealt with that long ago. I am healed; I feel just fine."

After counseling around Thanksgiving twelve years ago, I too, thought I was done. I kept saying to myself, "I'm done." Soon I realized I had a long way to go. After Christmas that year, I was barely functioning. I didn't know who the "new Janet" was or what she looked like, nor how to act, respond, or think. Where do you start when you are trying to discover who you might be?

I literally sat for six months. I was numb and in a daze. I couldn't process my thoughts, read my Bible, or pray. I said to the Lord, "I feel like a spider hanging from the ceiling; I am going to crash." In the quiet of my mind and heart I heard these words, "You have Me." Hearing those words changed my life. It was a slow process, but God became more personal than He ever had been, and my mental outlook began to change.

Slowly, God began to show me new ways of doing things. When I started thinking differently, my brain began to heal. God was healing me.

At the end of my first year of freedom, and looking at things from God's perspective, I saw that I was different than I had been at the beginning of the year.

Every year since has been another year of growth, renewal, strength, right thinking, and joy because my relationship with God has been more personal, and very different from what I believed before. I do not take it lightly. I trust Him more with the details of my daily living, and I am experiencing His presence in each day. I am intentional, speaking the truth. I recite verses God has given me for hope and strength.

Truth changed me. Abuse controlled my mind before I

knew what I was suffering from. Now truth is a new pattern, and my new way of life.

**My Purpose**

My purpose in writing this book is to share what experiencing God in everyday life looks like. God reveals himself, while Satan, the enemy, attacks and tries to destroy. He attacks because our guard is down, or because a new memory throws you a curve ball you were not expecting. A person cannot live on past victories. You must claim new ones. Practicing what you know and have heard makes you the victor.

My prayer is to help you identify the symptoms, be an overcomer, and thrive in your daily life, by helping you see what the process of healing looks like. It is not easy, but it's worth the effort.

This book is not for entertainment, and it is not for the fainthearted. It is written to let you know the raw truth of what many children suffer and carry into their adult life, limping along and trying to make life work. Healing takes time, tears, faith, courage, and prayer. You must become angry enough to fight, to regain what you lost. You must have tenacity and boldness to speak the truth. You must be vulnerable and share your story, not fearing what people think. Without God, it is impossible to walk the road to healing. Even though I have been a believer for many years, I have found that without facing the facts about sexual abuse, the pain and bondage of abuse do not go away.

Healing is a choice—an intentional decision one day at a time, one moment at a time. Through this book I walk alongside as you begin your healing journey. I hope to encourage you to trust God daily by learning how to face each day, and how to combat the attacks of Satan. My prayers are with you. God loves you. God is for you. Jesus died for you to give you life. Redemption is the reason I write.

I love God, I love Jesus for dying for my sins, and I love the Holy Spirit because he is my teacher. I offer to you what God has given to me—freedom and redemption. I believe you cannot have freedom without redemption. Redemption is God's story. In telling my story, I am telling you God's story. Without God's story, I do not have a story.

I am healing every day; healing never stops. It is a beautiful thing to heal, a gift. It is joy unspeakable.

*It is for freedom hat Christ has set us free. Stand firm, then, and do not let yourselves be burdened again by the yoke of slavery.* Galatians 5:1 NIV

If you have been sexually abused, use this book as a guideline to thrive. It's worth it. This whole process of living as a survivor is a daily thing.

I struggled in my inner world for years. Coming to the place of healing was such a gift. I have met many people on this same journey. My heart's desire is to help everyone I can.

**How I came to write this book.**

A few years ago, I went to my first Colorado Christian Writer's Conference to learn how to write a blog, never thinking I would become a writer. After attending for two seasons, I felt the call of God to write this book.

Knowing God, his purpose, having a voice, and having a desire to help others know the truth about sexual abuse have brought about this book. We must know the symptoms of sexual abuse, the emptiness and all the craziness that goes along with it. Knowledge helps set us free.

Does this mean I have it all figured out? No. I keep learning and reading. We need each other. We need community. I am here to pass on what God has taught me, to give you hope and courage to live in freedom. Freedom is too wonderful to keep to myself. I want everyone to know the beauty of freedom.

You may read this book from cover to cover or by topic, whichever is best for your learning. The white spaces on the sides are for your use, the music is to soothe your soul, and you may add your own verses and songs to your book.

I pray you do.

# MY STORY

My earliest memories of life are from when my family moved to a rented farm just a few miles south of the state line. I was four years of age, and I started having nightmares in this home. Just before my sixth birthday when I started first grade, I had the feeling that something was wrong with me. I didn't know what, but my child's mind wondered how I would ever be rid of the hovering feelings I could not understand.

I had two recurring unforgettable dreams which lasted into my late teens. The first was a monster knocking at an unlocked door that I was unable to hold shut. An arm came around the door, grabbing at me. I felt I would be devoured or killed. I woke up in paralyzing fear and hid under layers of blankets, afraid to go back to sleep for fear of the dream continuing.

Later a second dream began. I was sitting around a campfire with a hole in the middle. I could see another world revolving within the fire, and everything was ablaze. I was fearful of falling into the fire.

When I was ten, the fear of death gripped me. I prayed and begged God not to let me die.

Our family had always attended Sunday school and church. We had a wonderful teacher who made the Bible alive, and I loved Sunday School. I knew that when you died you either went to heaven or to hell, and I did not want to go to hell and burn. I was very afraid of dying.

These two dreams colored my life with fear, shame, insecurity, worthlessness, and uncertainty. I was unable to verbalize my feelings or make decisions. I felt contempt for myself, ambivalence, hopelessness, and revenge. It became my quest to find the answer to what was wrong with me at a very early age.

Growing up was hard for me; I had so many feelings I could not describe. I struggled in school, and I was afraid something bad would happen if I did something wrong. I didn't have the words to express what I felt. I didn't seem to have choices and wasn't allowed to voice my opinion.

To compensate, I always looked for something to fix myself. Nothing worked. I tried hard to be good and be nice. I thought, "If I do these things, life will be good." But it wasn't. I lived in a world of emotional pain. As a young child, I hit, kicked, and scratched to protect myself. My teachers said I had bad behavior. Nobody questioned why I acted that way. I was told, "You better be good, or else." Looking back, I wonder why no one questioned the sadness of this little girl.

While in counseling, this part of my story was revealed: I was sexually abused from age four to age twelve during the night while everyone was sleeping. The abuse became more frequent as I got older; I had many days I hated to see my dad come home at night after he was gone during the day. My hatred grew until I prayed that he would die in a car accident so I wouldn't have to ever see him again. I dreaded being around him. In the course of counseling at age sixty-one I had a horrendous flashback of how the abuse stopped.

I relived the night my oldest brother who was ten at the time heard my cries in the night and came to investigate. He caught my dad. The sexual abuse stopped, but he never stopped trying until the day I left home. However, the verbal, emotional, mental, and psychological abuse never stopped.

Because of the trauma of the event, I did not remember it, and I don't believe my brother remembered either. My brother died before I found out the truth of my story. I will never know.

I was the oldest of four and the only girl. My brothers and I went to a country school through eighth grade—my dad said an education was unnecessary for raising children and said I couldn't attend high school. I started to stand up for myself and fought back. I won, but I wasn't allowed to be involved in school activities and functions. I felt suffocated and left out.

On my eighteenth birthday, I moved out of the family home. My dad ranted and raged with cursing and told me that I had 'made my bed; now sleep in it.' I had no idea what he was talking about.

Because of health issues in the family, my continuing education after high school fell through; I was terribly disappointed. Instead, a job was attained for me that I was ill-suited for and I didn't do well. My dad bought me a car but wanted me to pay him back. He also wanted me to hand over the money I earned at my job. I fought back by resisting and invested my money, so it wasn't available to give to him. I felt like the black sheep of the family.

It was very convenient, a year later, to marry and move away. Both my husband and I moved away to escape. I had the opportunity to begin again at only eighteen years of age.

I had never been away from home and didn't know what homesickness looked like. Not having the vocabulary and being unable express my pain, I shut down, and this created explosive situations. Shutting down became a pattern for me.

To prove I was worthy, I overcompensated by staying busy. I worked from the moment I woke up until I crashed at night. I raised two children, worked part-time, went to church and Bible studies, belonged to organizations, and did things for people to prove myself worthy. I loved it all, but I didn't rest or play. I didn't know how. I was exhausted much of the time.

When we went home to visit—a seven-hundred-mile trip—I became a nervous wreck. I experienced stomach problem, bladder infections, and I felt fearful and nervous. I enjoyed everyone except my dad. He wouldn't look at or talk to me directly. He constantly gave me advice on minor situations. Nothing I did pleased him. No matter what I did, it wasn't enough. I was always glad to go back to Colorado.

I started going to counselors at age thirty-five. At age forty-nine, with counselor number ten, I was told that all my symptoms were related to childhood sexual abuse. Because of suppressing the painful trauma, I did not remember my abuse. I could not hear the words, and I said it was not true. The thought was so incomprehensible, so foreign; I did not think it was possible. Mentally I froze up. I denied it happened.

I suffered for another eleven years with health issues, sleep deprivation, anxiety, and weakness. I thought I would die. It was a living hell.

My daughter spoke up and said I needed to find out what I was dealing with. It was painful and humiliating, and it brought me to a crossroads. In a divine appointment, I met a counselor at church and went into counseling for the eleventh time in twenty-six years. I was told if I did not face the truth, I would get worse. In fear of dying of weakness and health issues, I chose to face the truth.

In processing after counseling, I realized my dad was the only one who made me afraid, criticized me at every turn, denied me things I wanted, was silent when I asked questions, and never answered me. I realized for the first time that I gave up every other person in my family just to get away from him. I lost so much, and it grieved me.

My dad occupied more mental real estate in my mind than anyone else. I was in mental bondage to him in my inner world. I played mental movies to prove my value to him, never saying the words out loud. I felt like a crazy woman. Facing the truth about the mental hold he had on me was monumental, and I felt angry at myself for not seeing it before. I was angry.

Going through counseling was both my worst year and my best year. I came to grips with the truth of abuse by my dad. My mind was blown away with the very thought of it—how abuse ruined and stole my life and my personality, and almost cost me my marriage. The anger put a fight in me to overcome.

The first childhood dream I mentioned revealed it was my dad who abused me. He sexually abused me for eight years, continuing emotional, spiritual, and verbal abuse until he died. Even when I married, he would call and threaten me. I found out later he never carried through with his threats—he had lied.

Later, as I was journaling, God revealed the answer to the second nightmare—I would "burn in hell" if I told about the abuse. I now knew why I was afraid of dying. How horrible! That lie dominated my life. My soul felt on fire with rage and anger. I finally understood what I didn't understand before. The lie was woven so tightly in the fibers of my life, controlling and dictating—it was the reason I took so long to learn the truth.

In time, by God's grace, I saw I was better off than he, a

man in bondage who never knew the truth of freedom himself. But now, I did. It took sixty-one years to learn the truth about the lies and abuse he inflicted on me. I saw the pain of his life, the secrecy, the silence. To me, it was worse than knowing I wasn't loved or valued by him. I no longer believe those lies. I became the free one. He is responsible for his actions. He never admitted any harm to me and never asked for my forgiveness. What happened to me was not my fault, but what I did with the harm was my sin. My forgiveness came in my confession of having hatred, revenge, malice, and trying by my own efforts to justify to myself that I was not a bad girl. I was set free from my sin by no longer believing the lies but the truth of who God said I was in Christ Jesus which is called redemption.

Redemption is the greatest gift, an eternal truth I hold in my heart and mind and soul.

*If you abide in My word, you are my disciples indeed. And you shall know the truth and the truth shall make you free.* John 8:31-32

I have been abiding in God's love. I have the tools to fight the spiritual warfare against my mind and body. Daily time with God is my refuge and my strength and my help in time of trouble. My relationship with Jesus Christ is precious to me. He set me free by teaching me to know who I am in Him.

## I Can Only Imagine – Mercy Me
https://www.youtube.com/watch?v=N_lrrq_opn

# DAY 1: GOD LOVES YOU

*But God demonstrated His own love toward us, in that while we were still sinners, Christ died for us.* Romans 5:8

*For God so loved the world that He gave His only begotten Son, that whosoever believes in Him should not perish but have everlasting life.* John 3:16

*The Lord has appeared of old to me saying: Yes, I have loved you with an everlasting love; therefore with lovingkindness I have drawn you.* Jeremiah 31:3

The world of abuse is a lonely world. It isolates you because you think you are the only one. You have been sworn to secrecy by your abuser. You are threatened, harmed, or manipulated into believing you are the cause of all that is going on between you. Fear keeps you from speaking or telling what is happening.

Secrecy is the enemy's best tool.
~Tom Parks

You may have heard about God's love many times, but you haven't believed. If God loved you, you wouldn't be in this mess. You have begged God many times to make it stop. It didn't. Where was God if he loved you so much? Or, you may never have heard that God loves or cares about you.

God gave every person free will, including the person who harmed you or is harming you. Abusers have a choice; they've chosen to use you, satisfying their own needs. You are in their grip; your innocence, dignity, personhood, and carefree happiness has been stolen, silencing you. You are a pawn, and they own you. The question is: Do you want to break the power the abuser has over you? Do you want to regain the things lost and get your life back?

**God has provided a way. Will you accept God's offer of love?** Will you trust a God who gave up His Son to give your life back to you? He paid a great price to free you from sin—your sin and those who sin against you.

We were all born into sin, we are all sinners.

*Surely, I have been a sinner from birth, sinful from the time my mother conceived me.* Psalms 51:5 NIV

*In this the love of God was manifested toward us, that God has sent His only begotten Son into the world, that we might live through Him. In this is love, not that we loved God but that He loved us and sent His Son to be the propitiation for our sins. Beloved, if God so loved us, we also ought to love one another.* 1 John 4:9-11

Abused people do not feel loved by anyone. Love is a foreign word to you; it is hard to imagine love. God loves everybody but you; you feel you are not worthy to be loved.

You have believed lies because the devil, Satan, wants to destroy you. He hates you and wants you to fail, get frustrated, and give up.

God loves you. Believe that God loves you. You cannot and will not love yourself unless you believe God loves you.

A dear friend of mine who has passed away used to say, "Let God love on you." If we reject God's love, nothing will change, and our heart is hardened. God *does* loves you. He will give you a soft heart, if you let him.

**Will you let God love you?**

I have listed the above verses for you to sit and soak in, absorb, think about, and savor. Allow yourself to feel the words. God wants you to know all Jesus came to offer you so that you can live in freedom. Own the words; they are yours.

Knowing the above verses has been and continues to be my reinforcement. I depend on them to know who I am in Christ and all He has provided.

What do you believe about God that causes you to want to give yourself to Him? (Select one of the verses above.)

What is true about God loving you?

_____
_____
_____
_____
_____
_____
_____
_____

*Father, I hear the words that you have loved me from the beginning. Wrap your arms around me right now. I am having a hard time believing; give me faith to believe and trust you. Amen.*

**How He Loves Us – David Crowder**
https://www.youtube.com/watch?v=GzfPHnoTo-o

# DAY 2: KNOW JESUS

*But those who wait on the LORD shall renew their strength; they shall mount up with wings like eagles, they shall run and not be weary, they shall walk and not faint.* Isaiah 40:31

Knowing Jesus as your personal Savior makes a big difference in reading this book, processing new information, and working toward freedom. Without Jesus, we do not have the guidance of the Holy Spirit. We, in ourselves, cannot do this work alone. Having been through counseling and saying we are healed is not enough. Every day is a new day. Some days we wake up in a deep hole, wondering if we will make it. We need encouragement on days like these. Depending on the Lord and His guidance through the Holy Spirit renews our strength.

In my years of helping and encouraging people in their healing process, I have had more than one person say to me, "Stop! This is too much work. I am not going there." Yes, this is work. It is emotionally exhausting work. It takes energy, margin and time. It takes prayer and intentional purpose every day to persevere and overcome. This is spiritual warfare.

When I was at the crossroads of my life, I looked forward to being healed, wondering what healing and freedom looked like. I hadn't been free a day in my life and I was over sixty years old. Looking back, all I saw was pain, agony, health issues, frustration, confusion, and nightmares. I was tired and exhausted. I was weak in body and mind, afraid that if I went back to doing what I had always done, I would die. My decision was to move forward and trust God with my future. I had no strength to stay where I was.

Whether you believe in God or not, you have chosen to read this book, and you have heard me say, "God loves you." Keep hearing that—God loves you! We cannot know God unless we acknowledge His way is the only way to know God personally. It is the way of the cross. *Jesus said to him, "I am the way, the truth, and the life. No one comes to the Father except through Me."* John 14:7

If you have never received Jesus Christ as your Savior, the good news is what He's done for you. Believe him.

The Bible tells us that all of us have sinned and cannot make it to heaven on our own; in fact, we deserve to die and be separated from God forever. God loved us so much, that He provided a way for us to have eternal life with Him. He sent His Son Jesus to take the punishment for our sin and give us His righteousness, so we can have eternal life instead of death. What a gift!

*For all have sinned and fall short of the glory of God.* Romans 3:23

*For the wages of sin is death, but the gift of God is eternal life in Christ Jesus our Lord.* Romans 6:23

*If you confess with your mouth the Lord Jesus Christ and believe in your heart that God has raised Him from the dead, you will be saved. For with the heart one believes unto righteousness, and with the mouth confession is made unto salvation.* Romans 10:9

Would you like to accept the gift God is offering you? You can do that right now by talking with God wherever you are, silently or aloud. Your prayer may go something like this:

*Lord Jesus, I know I have sinned. Please forgive me for all my sins. I believe you died on the cross and rose again to give me new life in and through you. I have tried to live my life by myself and it has not worked, I need you. Forgive me my sins, help me to know the truth about you and about the life that I might live in freedom. Amen.*

*Signature* _____
*Date* _____

If you have already received Jesus into your life, you may want to pray a prayer of renewal to the Lord Jesus:

*Lord Jesus, I want to come back into relationship with you. Forgive me for wandering my own way and not trusting in you. I am scared, and I do not know what to expect. I want you to guide me and give me direction. Amen.*

*Signature*_____
*Date*_____

*And this is the testimony: that God has given us eternal life, and this life is in His Son. He who has the Son has the life; he who does not have the Son of God does not have life.* 1 John 5:11-12

**Jesus Christ now lives inside you. He loves you and wants you to walk with Him.**

*Father, thank you that you are my Savior and friend, living in me with your Holy Spirit, walking with me in all my struggles and uncertainty. I have been lost and wandering. Forgive me. I want to be in relationship with you and follow your word, to live as a survivor and thrive. I want to be free and live in safety, trusting you. In Jesus name. Amen*

**Come Into My Heart Lord Jesus – Ve Louisiana**
https://www.youtube.com/watch?v=rCocp7dWSNU

# DAY 3: DISCOVER YOURSELF

*Then King David went in and sat before the Lord; and he said: 'Who am I, O Lord God? And what is my house, that You have brought me this far?* 2 Samuel 7:18

Like David, we are in the place we are because God brought us here. We are in this place with his plan to bless us.

It is important to develop good habits in our reading and writing and thinking, to discover the layers of our being. Journaling is key in our healing process. It gets thoughts out of our inner being , and it gives voice to the words not expressed. It may surprise you, revealing things hidden for a very long time.

The influences on our minds are profound. They affect what we believe about ourselves, how we think, what we say, and what we do. The foundation of these beliefs was formed in our early years. Being abused changed the foundation of good—and the image of God on our lives—into wrong beliefs and thoughts. We don't have the words to express our feelings because of the abuse and the shame.

There is difficultly in deciding between truth and lies, not knowing where to turn or what to do next, confusion, uncertainty. We think we are done, but we are only beginning.

In the place of discovering, give yourself time to describe your thoughts and feelings. Journaling is a key component. Start simple. It's your choice whether to write daily or when you have something that needs to be worked through. When you are uncertain or feeling uneasy, learn how to breathe deeply and exhale slowly as you think, giving yourself time to put the words together. Pause and ponder your words. Be kind to yourself for past or present feelings or actions. Say good words to and about yourself. Perhaps you are asking, "What does this mean?" Give yourself time to identify what it is you are feeling or thinking. Use the dictionary, write the meaning, grasp the meaning even if the word is familiar to you. This helps you in gaining new insight. Use a concordance to the Bible as well. The Hebrew and the Greek give depth and insight. Become a student for your own wellbeing.

Answering the questions presented to you is a key to defining what you are really thinking and feeling. At times, we are surprised by what we write. It is amazing how the pen reveals our true selves. The writing process will help you see yourself and give clarity.

Think through what you have written. Knowing yourself gives you confidence in speaking truth to yourself and others. Look at how it has affected you. How are you answering the question? Is it with anger, protection, avoidance, assumption? At times, we do not know how we are feeling until we answer the question presented. It is not a waste of time. It is necessary, the stepping-stones needed to give the correct words to what you believe.

Maybe nobody ever cared about how you felt before. If they showed an interest, you ignored them, feeling it didn't matter and assuming they didn't really care. Your feelings are very important to knowing who you are. You matter. You count. You are valuable in God's eyes. What you say and do has value.

**Do not expect to hurry this process—you have been in this place of harm for a long time, healing takes time.**

The feeling words list helps (see appendix). Take the time to read over this list. Select a word you are feeling right now, record it, and date it.

How does it feel to identify what you really feel?

_____
_____
_____
_____
_____
_____
_____
_____

As you do, you will get in touch with feelings that have been suppressed or ignored for a very long time.

This exercise of identifying and expressing the words will be a continuing part of giving your voice back to you, giving you confidence, and changing the countenance of your face. The person God created you to be is emerging from within your soul. You can breathe and feel alive. It feels good to be alive.

. . .

WHAT WORD or words have you chosen today?

_____
_____
_____
_____
_____
_____
_____
_____

As victims we are stuck. As survivors, the internal you is coming alive again. Keep up the patterns you are developing. Don't go back to the old way of thinking—discrediting and being hard on yourself. You have a choice to not slide back; you can choose to move forward just by thinking correctly and speaking the words. Also, speak the words of truth from God's Word, and recite the verses you have learned or a song you love. Look forward, not back.

*Let the words of my mouth and the meditation of my heart be acceptable in Your sight, O Lord, my strength and my Redeemer.* Psalm 19:14

*Trust in the Lord with all your heart and lean not on your own understanding; in all your ways acknowledge Him and He will direct your paths.* Proverbs 3:5-6

**Have you ever asked yourself "Who am I?" or "Why am I as I am?"** Journaling is one way to discover who you are. It is important to develop good habits in reading and writing and thinking to discover the layers of our being.

_____
_____
_____
_____
_____
_____
_____
_____

*Father, I pray you give me the words I haven't be able to say. Help me identify what I am feeling and be honest with myself, recalling Your word or a song in the moments I doubt. I pray to know who You created me to be, believing You and trusting not going back to my false belief of myself. I am a survivor because of who You say I am: Your beloved child. Thank you. Amen.*

**YouTube: Who Am I – Casting Crowns**
https://www.youtube.com/watch?v=mBcqria2wmg

## DAY 4: BIBLE READING

*All scripture is given by inspiration of God, and is profitable for doctrine, for reproof, for correction, for instruction in righteousness, that the man of God may be complete thoroughly equipped for every good work.* 2 Timothy 3:16-17

God wants to be in relationship with you. Relationships take time to nurture and grow. Reading our Bible is the way we get to know God, what He has done for us, and how He has done it. Taking time each day can be compared to meeting a new friend and getting to know them by spending time with them. Putting God first gives guidance and direction for the busyness of your day. Talk to Him during the day as you go about your business. It is your privilege.

Find a quiet place to read your Bible; ask for understanding of what you are reading. Ask God to show you what He wants you to see in His word. Start with one verse or with a few verses or with a chapter. One suggested reading is the book of Mark. Mark writes good news to people who are seeking and searching. You will draw encouragement and strength from the life and example of Jesus.

You can read through the Bible systematically or topically. Use the concordance and look up all the verses on the word you have selected. Find someone to give you guidance on how to use a Bible. Be curious about the following:

- Who is speaking?
- What is the application?
- Are there any principles to live by?
- Is there a commandment to live by?
- What is Jesus saying to you personally?

Read the passage as if Jesus is talking to you or wants you to know who He is. It is documented that writing your thoughts down on paper is healing for the mind. We are encouraged in Habakkuk 2:2 to *"write it down and make it plain, that he may run who reads it."* You are the writer and the reader; this is a visual picture of your personal adventure with God.

**Pouring out your heart and soul on paper is a very healing part of your journey.** Don't worry about grammar and spelling; just write. If a word or phrase jumps out and grabs your attention, underline it; ask God to show you what it means. (I call these "neon words;" they are like blinking lights. Check them out. Savor them.) Enter the date and the text you are reading, anything you want to remember.

This journal is for you, a safe place. At the end of the week, review what you have written. You will be surprised and encouraged by all you are learning. Writing is a great way to see what is really happening and to give insight into what is being taught through the Holy Spirit. It is how our own questions are answered.

*The LORD is my light and my salvation—*
  *whom shall I fear?*
*The LORD is the stronghold of my life—*
  *of whom shall I be afraid?*
*When the wicked advance against me*
  *to devour me,*
*it is my enemies and my foes*
  *who will stumble and fall.*
*Though an army besiege me,*
  *my heart will not fear;*
*though war break out against me,*
  *even then I will be confident.*
*One thing I ask from the LORD,*
  *this only do I seek:*
*that I may dwell in the house of the LORD*
  *all the days of my life,*
*to gaze on the beauty of the LORD*
  *and to seek him in his temple.*
*For in the day of trouble*
  *he will keep me safe in his dwelling;*
*he will hide me in the shelter of his sacred tent*
  *and set me high upon a rock...*
*Then my head will be exalted*
  *above the enemies who surround me;*
*at his sacred tent I will sacrifice with shouts of joy;*
  *I will sing and make music to the LORD.*
*Psalm 27:1-6*

Psalms and Proverbs have been my teacher and my guide, and have led me on paths of righteousness. God is there. He has given me confidence in who God says I am and how He protects me. He shows me my dependence on Him and on how to live. There are always times of disappointment, delays, moments when things happen, but through it all God has always been there.

> *To know wisdom and instruction, to perceive the words of understanding, to receive the wisdom of instruction, justice, judgement and equity; to give prudence to the simple, to the young man knowledge and discretion. A wise man will hear and increase in learning, and a man of understanding will attain wise counsel, to understand a proverb and an enigma, the words of the wise and their riddles. The fear of the Lord is the beginning of knowledge, but the fools despise wisdom and instruction.* Proverbs 1:2-7

Reading a chapter of Psalms or Proverbs regularly keeps me focused on how much God is involved in my life. Many are wonderful prayers to pray. I read the cross reference for clarity and validation on how to implement things into my life. I also memorize many verses to have as instant weapons of warfare against the enemy when he attacks at the least expected time.

God is so amazing in how He works and so timely—I love seeing God work. The assurance of His presence is there 24/7, ever present, powerful, and reassuring.

Write verses on three by five cards and carry them with you, reading them while waiting for a stop light or waiting in line. We need encouragement in difficult times and scripture is better than anything else, as it gives us a future and a hope.

Proverbs has thirty-one chapters; reading the Proverb for the current date is a good plan. If you miss a day, pick up with the date on the calendar and keep going. God does not care if you miss a day. He knows your heart, and He does not criticize, dock you, or shame you. Make an appointment with God in your daily schedule, and begin reading today. Never do tomorrow what you can do today.

Will you plan to read a Psalm or a Proverb daily?

Will you make a commitment today to read a chapter a day for thirty days to start a new habit?

Write your appointed time here:

When you finish, write your progress here:

_____

_____

_____

_____

_____

_____

_____

_____

*Father, I am so glad to have a Bible. Please give me understanding of what I read. Renew my mind. I will make an appointment to meet with you somewhere in my day, beginning to learn what you have for me and writing what you are teaching me. I look forward to meeting with you. Protect my time. I pray that I will read slowly and absorb the gift of your provision and love to me. Thank you. Amen.*

**Take Time to be Holy – Joseph Habedank**
https://www.youtube.com/watch?v=uVDzmEXBT34

# DAY 5: IDENTIFY THE WORDS

*A soft answer turns away wrath, but a harsh word stirs up anger. The tongue of the wise uses knowledge rightly, but the mouth of fools pours forth foolishness.* Proverbs 15:1-2

The first time I attended Journey group, I became acquainted with a new vocabulary. In my heart and mind, I would belittle myself for saying wrong words or words spoken out of place. I beat myself up for what I thought was inappropriate.

The workbook's "feeling list" of words described thoughts and feelings I was unaccustomed to. Being abused had shut down my mind and I didn't know how to think for myself. I was not comfortable expressing my thoughts; I was numb and silent. We were now encouraged to describe our feelings and thoughts. It scared me and awakened my spirit at the same time.

This may seem very elementary, but it is a new world of expression for someone coming out of abuse. Learning to identify words helps us think for ourselves. Naming them wakes up our spirit.

I made a list of the new words, my new language, in the front of my workbook to use as a reference. I realized the depth of my years of bondage when I was not able to describe how I felt.

It rocked my world to finally understand the meaning behind the feelings. It relieved my inner stress. I felt peace coming into my soul and found new ways to engage with expectations instead of resistance. I asked myself, "I wonder what it would look like if...?" I became curious and my world began to change.

There is freedom in describing feelings and having words to express ourselves. Our silence suppresses our feelings. Lack of words make us frustrated and angry; we become irritable. We are accused of not knowing anything or cooperating with our abuser, which shames us more and more. Shame silences us to a greater degree, and our hurt goes deeper and deeper. No one knows our heart or seems to care; we feel lost, hopeless, and alone.

New words open a world we did not know could be ours. Knowing what abuse looks like gives power back to you. Fight for yourself. Find help. Find a person of trust. Pray and ask God for protection and help.

*Pleasant words are like honeycomb, sweetness to the soul and health to the bones.* Proverbs 16:24

**Pleasant words calm our spirit, and we are less likely to become angry.** Anger comes out when we are afraid—we speak loudly, become defensive, and say words we wish we hadn't said. We feel unheard. Having a new selection of words calms us and makes a big difference in how we respond because we are able to say the right words.

*Be sober, be vigilant, because your adversary the devil walks around like a roaring lion, seeking whom he may devour.* 1 Peter 5:8

A new vocabulary opens your world to awareness, rest, and peacefulness. The restrictions and uncertainty dissipates. There is freedom in knowing the words for our feelings and having words to express ourselves.

What new words have you become aware of since reading this book?

_____
_____
_____
_____
_____
_____
_____
_____

*Heavenly Father teach me new words to renew my spirit. Forgive me for outbursts of anger that mask my self-defensiveness. Help me understand my hurts and identify my pain. Give me an understanding of new words that speak life to my spirit. Let the words of my mouth and the meditation of my heart be acceptable in Your sight, O Lord, my strength and my Redeemer. Amen.* Psalm 19:14

**Learning to Lean – Heritage Singers**
https://www.youtube.com/watch?v=7dHBtdsAGW8

# DAY 6: NAME IT

*Therefore humble yourselves under the mighty hand of God, that He may exalt you in due time, casting all your care upon Him, for He cares for you.* 1 Peter 5:6-7

*Cast your burden on the Lord, and He shall sustain you; He shall never permit the righteous to be moved.* Psalm 55:22

Not remembering abuse is common in children who are abused at an early age. I was so programmed with fear to not speak unthinkable words that I could not say the words. My counselor had me journal each week, giving me a specific topic to write about. When he asked questions about what I wrote, I could answer the questions, and I remembered. I didn't really forget. It was all there—repressed and very tangled up. Each week when I spoke more words of my story, I sat in unbelief of the horrors I went through. It seemed impossible. I raged with curses and thought of murdering a dead man. Then, I felt guilty for thinking such thoughts. I couldn't imagine this happening to little children, but it does. Every day.

God gave me wonderful promises for healing from this

great trauma. "Cast" is an active verb that means "to cause to move or send forth." Cast it onto Jesus. He carries my burden —and me—in the process. I was intentional about applying Scripture dealing with the magnitude of it all.

How long has it been since you allowed yourself to remember the harmful thing that happened to you?

What do you do when old memories start to surface?

Do you stuff them back down into the deepest part of your memory?

___

**A necessary step in healing is say the words, name the harm done, and the memories associated with it.** We see it and handle it. Naming it gives us the ability to be angry, sad, and grieve the loss. All of these are very necessary for getting the poison out of our system, and allowing healing to occur.

The truth is before us. What we believe about ourselves is, "it was my fault," "I caused it to happen." Not true. It is a lie. Cast off the lie.

What takes the place of a lie?

Truth.

Will you accept truth?

Find the truth. God's Word exposes the lies you believe. Write it down. You must go through the pain to be released or you will not be released. The pain must be dealt with. It gives courage to go to the next step. Recording your words is evidence that God is faithful to do what he says.

Tools to help face the truth are:

- journaling
- prayer
- Scripture reading
- sharing with a trusted friend

**Use the powerful truth of writing in your journal. It is proven evidence that God is at work, healing you.**

It has also been proven that writing helps to define, process, and give clarity. Writing your story gives you the opportunity to record your feelings and questions. Your memory is renewed—filling in the gap of things buried deep in the sub-conscious.

**Memory will also cause triggers. Triggers scare us. Keep persevering—they unlock secrets we are otherwise unable to find.**

You are lancing the infected wound of stuffed pain; the poison must be drained. Unless the wound is drained, we will not heal.

You will continue to have memories come to mind after years of healing. Do not be discouraged; it is an ongoing process. Overcoming the trauma of what we endured takes time, but you will keep learning and growing. It's very freeing.

Also, be in prayer. Ask God to reveal the event, the trauma, the place, the person involved, and the words spoken to know what you are dealing with. It's hard to know truth, but you must know it to heal. Ask the Lord to give you Scripture. Ask the hard questions for strength and courage to face them. Do not be afraid. Speak the truth about your painful events. Unless you say the words, as hard as they are to say, you cannot be set free. We grow through pain. Remember, God is in partnership with you through this learning and growing process. He wants you to have health and wellness more than you do. He is with you, guiding you and leading you where He knows you need to be.

*I will instruct you and teach you in the way you should go; I will guide you with my eye.* Psalm 32:8

I am repeating things because they are important to hear frequently. Name the issues you are dealing with. Look for books* that can help you learn about your mind, soul, and body. Be curious, alert, and stimulate your brain. You are gaining knowledge, finding a voice, and defining terms to give you hope and confidence.

Do you have a friend of your same gender with whom you can confide? If not, ask the Lord to provide one, because you will be incredibly blessed. A trustworthy friend can walk this journey with you, listen without judgment, pray with you, and encourage you when you're afraid.

*Ask, and it shall be given to you; seek, and you will find; knock and it will be opened to you.* Matthew. 7:7

*And you will seek Me and find Me, when you search for Me with all your heart.* Jeremiah 29:13

I sought God at every turn. I could not have done it without seeking Him and his Word. He is my anchor. The road to wellness—spiritual and mental—comes from right thinking and dependence on God. When I come to a place of not knowing what to do, I stand still. I ask God, "What do I do next?" I wait expectantly in my spirit until I sense His Spirit directing me. Being still physically and mentally calms and quiets my spirit. This can be done anytime, anyplace, without anyone knowing a decision-making process is going on.

Name all the things that are lies. Seeking and believing the truth is a blessed place to be. We cannot do this by ourselves or without God's help. We crash and burn when we solely depend on ourselves.

_____
_____
_____
_____
_____
_____
_____
_____

I failed and picked myself up many times before I got to the place of being in relationship with and reliant on Jesus. He is my friend and savior. Reliance on Him is my strength and peace.

*Jesus, help me to name the harm and identify the lies. Give me words to write and the words I have a hard time saying, as well as the clarity to see my story and the trauma I faced. Give me a friend to walk with me, to listen to me, and to pray for me. Give me faith to believe and strength to walk in the light of truth.*

*Thank you for caring for me in the smallest details of my life. In Your name I pray, amen.*

### No One Ever Cared or Me Like Jesus
https://www.youtube.com/watch?v=P1TxJH

(*Book list is found in the back of this book.)

# DAY 7: FINDING YOUR VOICE

*They walk all over your people, God, exploit and abuse your precious people. They take out anyone who gets in their way; if they can't use them, they kill them.* Psalm 94:4 MSG

When someone is abused by another person, their value and identity are destroyed with lies, their hearts are wounded, and their spirit is crippled. Their lives are forever changed.

*A wholesome tongue is a tree of life, but perverseness in it breaks the spirit.* Proverbs 15:4

This ad has been on TV and in our local newspaper in times past: The child is covering their face with a fake smile to hide the pain and turmoil. They may be sworn to secrecy or told that terrible things will happen to family members if they tell. Their world is a mass of confusion. Their mind is unable to sort out what happened and they cannot tell what they are feeling.

As a result, they may blame themselves, many times protecting the abuser. The child feels so alone. They do not have the vocabulary to speak about their trauma. This is called childhood sexual abuse.

When a child loses their voice, who will believe a child saying things they shouldn't know? Who will listen, and whom can they trust? The child loses their identity and their dignity. They are in a world of aloneness and isolation. The person they were created to be has no opportunity to grow and become a healthy adult.

While in counseling, there were times I didn't think I could go on. It all seemed too much. I felt at times I was crazy, and everything felt so mixed up. Sorting out the lies and finding the truth were hard. At one point, I tried to hurry the process, but it only caused more confusion. As I processed one memory followed another, I saw the picture and pattern of abuse. One memory upheld the other for clarity and it all made crazy sense. I saw the severity of the harm done, how twisted and sordid the behavior was, and its crippling effects.

It was mind-boggling to believe a parent could harm their own child in such a destructive way. But it happens all too often with devastating results.

**Healing and being able to properly express myself came in stages. Looking back, I realized my healing manifested in increments of a day, a week, a month, six months, a year and years.** Having a voice became a powerful part of me; I gained my personhood back. Self-worth began to grow, dignity was emerging, and I began to feel life in my soul. I felt like a flower growing in a garden, tended to, nurtured, watered, cared for, and slowly coming into bloom.

Your voice is how you feel, how you think, how you relate, how you respond. A person needs all this to express themselves. Your voice is who you are; it is the beauty God uniquely created in you to be a person. It is an amazing gift to know and experience.

When I finally was able to see it all, I wanted to sing and dance. It's such a great moment of hilarity, music, and laughter. Nothing can take its place. I carry it wherever I go. I love it; it is wonderful to live and have life.

One of the first steps toward healing is the day you share your story. It is the day you move forward.

In a recent article on the Broncos in the Denver Post a few weeks ago, I found this quote about Coach Cutliffe talking with Peyton Manning when he was injured late in 2014. He had been playing injured and the article spoke about the conversations they had about it. Manning arrived at Duke at the beginning of the year without any lingering effects of his quad injury because he had been in training to overcome the injury. Cutliffe said, "He (Manning) believes in it, and we certainly do, that in life as well as football, nothing stays the same—whether it is a relationship or anything else. You're either getting better or worse.'" Payton chose to heal.

Whether it is an injury of the body or the soul, we must choose to get better. Finding my voice has given me so much clarity in life, as well as a passion for living and speaking truth to myself and others. Choose life; choose to get better.

*The thief comes only to steal and kill and destroy; I have come that they may have life, and have it to the full.* John. 10:10 NIV

Wherever you are in the stages of healing, you must put words to your story and to your feelings, building your vocabulary to identify your trauma, for continued release. You will continue to put words to new memories or triggers. Go there, find the root cause, name the pain. Identify the root, and speak the truth to your heart and life. Only then can we move on to greater freedom.

*It is for freedom that Christ has set us free. Stand firm, then, and do not let yourselves be burdened again with the yoke of slavery.* Galatians 5:1 NIV

**Any trauma or any abuse is slavery. We become slaves to the lies and to our beliefs; we are in our own prison.** It is time to know the truth, to open the prison doors, and to walk out in the freedom.

*Today, Father, I pray I can see the truth of the bondage and lies I have believed. I want to walk out of my own prison. Give me the courage to stand firm, to walk with you in this freedom, and to learn to live again. Thank you for truth. Amen.*

**He Knew Me Then – Dallas Holm**
https://www.youtube.com/watch?v=JRzJV8S_sok

# DAY 8: A SAFE PLACE

*Be sober, be vigilant, because your adversary the devil walks about like a roaring lion, seeking whom he may devour.* 1 Peter 5:8

Living as a survivor of sexual abuse includes surviving the crime of rape. Rape victims feel the same things as a sexually abused person does regarding how they think and feel about themselves. After we learn to speak the truth and identify the things we feel and believe, the enemy, Satan, will do everything in his power to get us back to the place of living as victim again – feeling uncertain, ugly, dirty, worthless, and a host of many other things to keep you from living a victorious life in Christ Jesus.

Jesus Christ wants you to live in freedom in your mind, spirit, and soul. Unless you build a relationship with Jesus daily, you will lose your grip on the truth and begin to believe the lies again.

I, along with many other survivors, have been sucked into being a victim when I let my guard down, forget, don't sleep, or get tired. It is easy to slip into 'victim mode' again.

Remember, we are in warfare with the enemy. He loves to deceive us and destroy us. Know who he is; keep alert for his schemes.

Survivors need daily encouragement from God's Word to thrive and to gain the victory in the events that surprise us. These surprises include triggers, words other people say, sounds, smells, expressions, story lines in movies, vulgar words, or cursing.

**Know it is okay to be where you are. Practice what you learn; be in God's word. Put it to work for you; prove it.**

*Whatever you have learned or received or heard from me or seen in me – put it into practice. And the peace of God will be with you.*
Philippians 4:9 NIV

*If we say that we have fellowship with Him, and walk in darkness, we lie and do not practice the truth.* 1 John 1:6

Doing the work and seeking to live as a survivor is a moment by moment task. Give yourself margin; it takes energy and time to think and process. Take walks, don't binge, drink enough water, eat right, and get enough sleep.

Invite your trusted friend to read this book with you. Read the Scriptures together and pray. It is important to have a few guidelines in this relationship to ensure safety and trust:

- have confidentiality
- do not judge each other
- do not use abusive language
- guard against offending the other person; they may have heard you wrong or had an expectation you did not meet

- clear the air about the misunderstanding; take responsibility for your words and actions
- do not tell another person how to feel; instead, the question should be, 'How do you feel?'
- listen and offer words of encouragement

Answering the questions will help you progress to the next phase in your healing. Not finding resolution will keep you from the answers you need to progress to the next stage. Take your time—think through until you have an answer. Do not bypass the question. You need the answers to overcome, to understand your story.

There may be apprehension on your part for your lack of words or fear. It is all a part of the symptoms of abuse. You are in a good place; keep moving forward.

I am a fellow traveler. My passion is to be your friend, letting you know **you are not alone**. There are thousands of men and women in this same place. I want to encourage you that this is attainable. Maintaining our freedom is a privilege every day as we practice the truths, learning to thrive.

We suffer because defending ourselves harms us as we continue to hide the secrets we have endured. God is the Healer; my prayer is for you to see who you are and what you believe about yourself. I cannot emphasize this enough.

Our biggest fear is someone finding out our story, blaming us, or thinking badly of us, and rejecting us. It shuts us down and puts us into isolation. Do not let this stop you. You must tell your story. It is not in your head; it's real. Your body knows it. It is not your fault—get help and come out of this horrible lie.

Describe the fearful feelings you have right now (numbness, denial, anxiety, nervousness, anger, uncertainty) and the fearful beliefs (I am stupid, I am lazy, nobody will believe me).

_____
_____
_____
_____
_____
_____
_____
_____

I found it helpful to date my entries because it is encouraging when looking back. Most of us cannot see our progress, and it will be helpful for you to read your journal time to time to see how far you have come.

**It takes courage to look fear in the face, to speak the words, to know what you are overcoming. Be bold—name it! Be courageous.**

> *Come to Me, all you who are weary and burdened, and I will give you rest.* Matthew 11:28 NIV

Ask God to help you. He loves it when you ask.

> *Father give me the words I do not know. Help me be in a safe place to learn, grow, and heal. Give me a safe person to walk with me. Give me the courage to see where I am and the boldness to speak the words I know are true. This is a hard road to travel. I know you are with me. Strengthen me with your might and power. I trust you, Jesus. Amen.*

**You Are My Hiding Place – Selah**
https://www.youtube.com/watch?v=_dRoHotAYT8

## DAY 9: CALL ON ME

*Call to Me, and I will answer you, and show you great and mighty things, which you do not know.* Jeremiah 33:3

Charles Swindoll once said, "My favorite verse is the one I am reading." This is true for me as well. This morning, Jeremiah 33:3 came to mind. Memorizing this verse years ago, I claimed this verse by writing my name in front of it. God was talking to Jeremiah while he was shut up in prison. Verse two says, "Thus says the Lord, who made it, the Lord, who formed it to establish it (The Lord is His name.)" I felt I was in prison too—my own prison, not knowing how to get out or if I could.

In Strong's Concordances we find that the Hebrew word 'call' (*qara* #7121) means: "to call out to someone; to cry out; to address someone; to shout; to speak out; to proclaim." Sometimes *qara* means, "to name something," that is, to call it by its name, as God did when He called the light "day" and the darkness "night." (Genesis 1:5)

**Naming it starts the healing.**

I was aware of God in my younger days and called on the

Name of the Lord many times. At that time, I was unaware of what I was dealing with, but God met me in my uncertainty with the Scriptures I had memorized. As I would recite them, they gave me strength and courage to keep moving forward in my trust and faith in God. I never tire of going back to read a verse even though I know it by heart. When I use the verses as a prayer or ask questions about it, it is always fresh and new. He has revealed many things I would never have seen if I hadn't called out in prayer and asked. It is a practice I never stop doing.

I started going to Bible studies in my mid-twenties, having an unquenchable thirst for truth and knowledge of who God was. God taught me, and He used His Word in my life; He is my strength. I look back now and am so blessed by God's answers to many prayers. I am thankful for wonderful Bible studies, Bible study teachers, leadership training seminars, authors of books and concordances. I found encouragement and believed and did what the Word of God said. God is my teacher. I am in His classroom; He has equipped me and continues to this day

*You will keep him in perfect peace, whose mind is stayed on you. because he trusts in You. Trust in the Lord forever, for in YAH, the Lord is everlasting strength.* Isaiah 26:3-4

*For the word of God is living and powerful, and sharper than any two-edged sword, piercing even to the division of soul and spirit, and of joints and marrow, and is a discerner of thought and intents of the heart. And there is no creature hidden from His sight, but all things are naked and open to the eyes of Him to whom we must give account.* Hebrews 4:12-13

*As you therefore have received Christ Jesus the Lord, so walk in*

*Him, rooted and built up in Him and established in the faith, as you have been taught, abounding in it with thanksgiving, beware lest anyone cheat you though philosophy and empty deceit, according to the traditions of men, according to the basic principles of the world, and not according to Christ. For in Him dwells all the fullness of the Godhead bodily; and you are complete in Him, who is the head of all principalities and power.*
Colossians 2:6-10

**Through all my years of not remembering about the abuse done to me, God taught me about himself.** He gave me peace when I was hard on myself for not living up to my unmet expectations. My heart was a sponge for knowing God. It caused me to be curious, to seek a better way of living in my inner spirit. God has a way of guiding us to the things we need when we call on Him and ask for help. God loves it when we call on Him.

**We enlarge our faith by seeking after God and asking Him what the desire of His heart is for us.** Our hearts, minds, and lives change when we trust God, desiring His ways. Life is no longer status quo. We are in a new place, thinking and acting differently. We speak to the wrong that confronts us. We say "no" to things we had no power to say "no" to before. We learn to stand firm in what we believe and experience as true, living in a "new place."

We are no longer alone; fear is surrounded by the true words we are speaking and no longer has a grip on us. Our actions reveal our confidence in the One who redeemed us. We have faith to stand. **Saying "no" to controlling people gives our voice back. This is not done out of anger but out of love for ourselves, because we know God loves us.** God created us to be who He designed us to be, not puppets for someone else to control. Let us not insult Him by hating ourselves. We are a person of value. God does not create junk. We must know this to stand firm and believe Him.

Calling on God is our privilege, and God is honored by our calling on Him. He has been waiting for us to call on Him. He will show us great and mighty things, greater than what we can imagine for ourselves. Trust Him.

Are you calling on God to show you great and mighty things?

What has He shown you?

If not, what would you ask God for today?

_____

_____

_____

_____

_____

_____

_____

_____

My heart's desire is for you to grow stronger daily by calling on Jesus, who reveals what God the Father says to him. Jesus will show you the Father's heart. He loves you and wants you to be in relationship with Him. God wants you to experience His love.

*Father, thank you for giving me your Word. Thank you for letting me know I can call upon your name and that you will answer me. Give me the faith to believe you and trust you to provide what I need. I will write my name in front of the promises you give me. I pray your Word sinks deep into my bones and marrow, and that I will believe what you say. I want to be rooted and built up in you. In Jesus' name, amen.*

## I Will Run to You – Hillsong
https://www.youtube.com/watch?v=FpNruTıt_dw

# DAY 10: MY CONFIDENCE IS IN CHRIST

*Being confident of this very thing, that He who has begun a good work in you will complete it until the day of Jesus Christ.* Philippians 1:6

*But those that wait upon the Lord shall renew their strength; they shall mount up with wings like eagles, they shall run and not be weary, they shall walk and not faint.* Isaiah 40:31

God used these verses to make me strong when I was weak and kept me focused. They reminded me that He would strengthen me until the day He would come back to get me from this earth. I keep my mind on the promises God has given me.

I could be above my circumstances, not because I was able, but because He put me there and gave me the strength to do it. I overcame one issue, one problem, at a time.

Our thoughts and minds are in a rut with old messages and beliefs. We think about them so much, going around and around and around until the rut is deep in our brain. We cannot seem to get out of these ruts, but we climb out of them, one rut at a time.

**Knowing scripture pulls us out of the ruts; memorizing keeps our confidence in the Lord Jesus and allows scripture to come to mind when we need it.** He gives peace, so we can run and not be weary, able to walk and not faint. No matter where we are or what we are doing, we can keep our mind on the promises of God's Word.

Practicing God's Word in our minds while doing other things, keeps us focused. This is the work of the Holy Spirit—knowing God's promise that He is faithful until He returns gives us hope so we can press on.

Seeking God in prayer and applying His promises gives us victory. *I press toward the goal for the prize of the upward call of God in Christ Jesus* (Philippians 3:14). Having my eye on eternity has kept my mind on the goal.

**God keeps His promises, so we must keep ours.** When we work on keeping our promises, we overcome, and our mind gets us out of the ruts of wrong thinking and wrong doing. We overcome because Jesus overcame for us on the cross. He arose from the grave to break the power of sin and death. Because He did, we can overcome.

Do you want to get out of the rut of wrong thinking?

What wrong thoughts are in your thinking?

What promises will you hold onto to win the battle?

_____

_____

_____

_____

_____

_____

_____

_____

If this seems like hard work, that's because it is. It is no small thing. Your spiritual health depends on it. However, it becomes a way of life. It's for good reason we repeat things. We must hear something seven times to be able to make it a habit, to make it a part of our lives, and to put it into practice. The enemy wants to destroy you, wants you to fail, and he does not stop at seven times. Every little thing makes a difference. Little things become big. The small events in life teach us deep lessons of faith. Lessons add up to big things because they change how we respond; they change our thought processes and our desires. By not changing, we will do what we have always done and get the same results as we have always gotten. We need new patterns of living as survivors. It is a choice.

Write down any thoughts or questions and pray over them. God will answer you, so be intentional in asking Him, and you will see the progress you are making. It is important to see His hand moving in your life, accomplishing what only He can do through you. My prayers are with you as you journey on the victory road.

_____
_____
_____
_____
_____
_____
_____
_____

*Lord Jesus, today I confess: I want to give up because it seems so hard. I pray that I will put my confidence in you. Help me cling to your promises, and make me strong to overcome and crawl out of the rut I am in. Help me to keep my eyes on the goal for the prize of the upward call of God in Christ Jesus. Amen.*

### I Saw the Lord – Dallas Holm
https://www.youtube.com/watch?v=OofwolRXoEs

# DAY 11: EVERY DAY IS A NEW DAY

*Through the Lord's mercies we are not consumed, because His compassions fail not. They are new every morning; great is Your faithfulness.* Lamentations 3:22-23

Every day that you open your eyes to the morning sun is a blessed day. You have another day to walk with the Lord, another day to trust Him in all the moments He is bringing you. It is an opportunity to see God in action in your life. You can choose what and how you think; you have a voice to express it. You can act out all that God has taught you in His Word by how you demonstrate His love to those you live and work with.

Things may happen today you have never experienced before. Will you stop long enough to ask His wisdom on how to respond and what to say or will you make decisions and speak in haste? The unexpected happens: illness, job loss, fallout with a loved one. Who will you turn to? Who will give you comfort and guide you on this unknown path?

**We have a choice on how to think and respond.**

*Pleasant words are like a honeycomb, sweetness to the soul and health to the bones.* Proverbs 16:24

Will you depend on what you read and learned in God's Word to give you strength for the moment, for the decisions to be made?

**Applying God's truths will change your life. It does not matter what others say or do, but what you do.** The ripple effect of your words and actions today makes a difference in how you make tomorrow's decisions. Every day you choose to honor Jesus, you are honoring Him who created you. There is only one "you" in this world; God has ordained your life for a purpose only you can fill.

Will you submit to God's plan for your life?

_____
_____
_____
_____
_____
_____
_____
_____

*For I know the thoughts that I think towards you, says the Lord, thoughts of peace and not of evil, to give you a hope and a future. Then you will call upon Me and go and pray to Me and I will listen.* Jeremiah 29:11-12

Even if you are from a multiple birth, or you look like someone, **no one is exactly like you.**

*For You formed my inward parts; You covered me in my mother's womb. I will praise You, for I am fearfully and wonderfully made. Marvelous are Your works, and that my soul knows very well.*
Psalm 139:13-14

Every day is a new day; it makes a difference how you do life. You can choose; speak words of life to yourself and others. You are uniquely designed by God just to be you. He has a plan for you; depend on Him, and He will perform it. Seek God and His ways; He is waiting for you.

God put His glory in you. It can only be seen if you allow Him to conform you to His image. There will be peace in your heart and joy on your face when you come to this place. It will happen. I have seen it in many people's lives who have come through all of this. They are different and beautiful people, transformed and living in freedom.

God is the Giver of good gifts; He wants you to receive the gifts He has planned for you. Only when you allow Him will you know and see it for yourself. This is truly a gift from God —praise will come to your mouth. It's a blessed day when these things occur.

*Father today is a choice to live and honor you. It is a new day. You made me for a purpose. I want to fulfill that purpose by seeking you today and trusting you to show me from Your Word. Whatever portion of Scripture I read, let me hear your voice. Fill me with your strength, however small it may be—a beginning of you shaping and molding me to your image. Thank you for loving me and caring enough about me to reveal yourself to me. Amen.*

## Day by Day – On Screen Lyrics
https://www.youtube.com/watch?v=AzrhqjzQCi4

# DAY 12: LIFE IS MESSY

*Bring my soul out of prison, that I may praise Your name; the righteous shall surround me, for You shall deal bountifully with me.* Psalm 142:7

Did you ever think other people's lives were all orderly and yours was so messy? I did. I thought other people had life all together, had figured it out, and didn't have a care in the world. How wrong I was.

Everyone has a messy life, because nothing is ever perfect or simple or easy. We all learn to walk a new way when we live as a survivor.

I am amazed how God has shaped the messy events in my life and has made them into something beautiful. I cannot even imagine how He did it, but He did. He used failures, and discouragements, pain and trials, school and teachers, jobs and bosses to shape me into the person He knew I could be. He used friends and Bible studies, authors and books. He uses everything for His good and glory.

Through living as a survivor, we learn that God does care,

that He wants us to be victorious. He shows us how to overcome with these things:

- Read His word and believe what He says
- Pray
- Trust
- Rest
- Practice what He says
- Memorize and repeat to yourself His promises as many times a day as needed
- Take care of yourself
- Know your identity in Christ
- Be in a Bible study
- Include the things you will read in this book

**Because life is messy, we need community with others and validation with those who share our stories.** Don't give up. He brings us to this place to give hope and freedom.

Can you look back and wonder how God has shaped your life? He brings big and small events, and everything is put into place by God to make this life. No matter what has happened, God can use it for good.

**We all have a story to tell. We can help someone else who is walking a similar path.**

Who has God brought into your life to reveal their story to you? They are God's gift to you; you are not alone. Together you can encourage and build one another up.

*It is for freedom that Christ has set us free. Stand firm, then, and do not let yourself be burdened again with the yoke of slavery.*
Galatians 5:1 NIV

No matter how messy our life is, God has a plan for each one of us. It's what we do with our messiness, the help we seek, and our desire to change that makes a difference. Suffering abuse is a hard life, a horrendous life that no one should have to live through. We put ourselves in a prison to survive and to protect ourselves, a prison that keeps us isolated. **I encourage you to find out the truth of what sexual abuse does and walk out of that prison.**

God puts the random pieces of life together to weave together a beautiful story of redemption. God has brought me a long way and has given me new joy, a new life. My hope is to pass it on to you.

Healing is not easy, but it is worth the effort. Seek God, trusting Him to help you stand firm in faith as you face each day. Be encouraged as you see God revealing Himself and experience His presence. Know that God loves you; God is for you. Jesus died that you may have life and have it abundantly (John 10:10).

Learn the symptoms, fight for yourself, stand up and be heard. Find the person God created you to be, valued and loved for God's glory.

> *Lord Jesus, take the mess of my life and use it for something good. I do not know how you will do it, but I believe you. Set me free from wrong beliefs about myself. I pray to believe that I have value despite all that has happened to me. You died to save me from the sin that bound me and you set me free. Jesus, thank you. Amen.*

**Lord You Know – Riana Nel**
https://www.youtube.com/watch?v=-khkWMcJ2mk

# DAY 13: IT IS NOT YOUR FAULT

*When my father and mother forsake me; then the Lord will take care of me. Teach me Your way, O Lord, and lead me in a smooth path, because of my enemies. Do not deliver me to the will of my adversaries; for the false witnesses have risen against me, and such as breathe out violence. I would have lost heart, unless I had belied that I would see the goodness of the Lord in the land of the living.* Psalm 27:10-13

**Sexual abuse is not your fault.** Most people who are sexually abused blame themselves and carry the guilt of what happened to them. It is not ours to carry. The blame lies on the one who abused us. Abusers and predators are very good at manipulating us into believing we are the ones who caused the shame of abuse.

The results of shame are long lasting and detrimental. We blame ourselves, and it sucks us into a world of silence and isolation. It affects every area—our thoughts, actions, words, responses, reactions, plans, vocations, spouses, how we live, where we live—everything.

It may take us years to face the reality of what happened to us. Some have never faced the truth of what happened, living out their lives believing the lies. Don't fall into this trap of your abuser and of the world.

> *These things I have spoken to you, that in Me you may have peace. In the world you will have tribulation; but be of good cheer, I have overcome the world.* John 16:33

We do indeed, have tribulation.

I was locked into the world of tribulation for sixty-one years. My counselor identified it by my behavior, giving the clues of what was going on inside—defensiveness, perfectionism, how I dressed, insecurities, my shame, indecisiveness. It all brought to light my pain. Even though I didn't remember the abuse, my actions and my body did. What I said and did revealed the truth. Being asked the right questions, I was able to tell my story.

I was angry at what I believed about myself, the shame I carried, the blame, the guilt, the injustice. What does a person do with themselves when they realize they have been used, that they were used as a scapegoat for a life of lies and loss? How does a person get back what was lost? It didn't seem bearable. I wanted to scream, hit, kick, and kill. But who would I hit, kick, or kill? My abuser was dead. Yes, my heart wanted to kill. My heart screamed. What is enough revenge for a lifetime of loss? Who would pay for the injustice?

> *He is the Rock, His work is perfect; for all His ways are justice, a God of truth and without **injustice**; righteous and upright is He.* Deuteronomy 32:4

> *Yield now, let there be no **injustice**! Yes, concede, my righteousness still stands!* Job 6:29 *Beloved, do not avenge yourselves,*

*but rather give place to wrath; for it is written, "**Vengeance** is Mine, I will repay," says the Lord.* Romans 12:19

*You answered them, O L<small>ORD</small> our God; You were to them God-Who-Forgives, though You took **vengeance** on their deeds.* Psalm 99:8

I knew all these verses. I had to believe the truth of what God said. I also knew I was to forgive. It was hard. I wanted to hang on to the hate and anger; it took time to let go. I was paying a price by hanging on, because it owned me. It came in increments of time. Unless I forgave it would continue to own me. I was paying the price with all my hate, anger, and revenge.

*And **forgive** us our debts, as we **forgive** our debtors... "For if you **forgive** men their trespasses, your heavenly Father will also **forgive** you. But if you do not **forgive** men their trespasses, neither will your Father **forgive** your trespasses.* Matthew 6:12, 14-15

**God is very gracious in how He loves us—with kindness, grace, and forgiveness.**

He knew my pain. I also knew I had sinned by hating, being angry, and wanting vengeance. For God to forgive me, I had to forgive.

Forgiving is not easy, but we must. Spiritual work, mental assent, and the truth worked in my heart; my heart is healing day by day. I am still forgiving as I remember new events. Forgiving is ongoing; healing is ongoing.

You might say "It's too much work" or "I can't go there." But, really? Too much work? Being in your own prison is a life sentence on its own. Do you really want to condemn yourself to your own prison for the rest of your life?

I couldn't go there. I had been in my own prison for sixty-one years—it was long enough. I love Psalm 142:7: *Bring my soul out of prison, that I may praise Your name; the righteous shall surround me, for You shall deal bountifully with me.*

I wanted God to bring my soul out of prison because He had set me free and I wanted to praise him for doing it. I am righteous not because of whom I am, but because of who Jesus is. He died for me to set me free. He is righteous; He gave me life eternal. It is something to shout about. You can be free, too. You do not have to pay the price for your sexual abuse or have shame and guilt. It is not yours to carry; give it back to the one who caused the abuse. It is his shame not yours. He violated you; give it back where it belongs.

**God is the Giver of life and breath; sin is the taker of life and gives death.** You have a choice. I pray you will take life and freedom and joy and everything God has to offer you. I love you dear reader. I know your pain and want you to be set free.

I wonder who God created you to be?

Would you be willing to trust Him and find out?

———————————————————————
———————————————————————
———————————————————————
———————————————————————
———————————————————————
———————————————————————
———————————————————————
———————————————————————

*Father, you are so gracious to let me know the truth about sexual abuse. Give me the courage to believe it is not my fault. I want forgiveness to be able to unload this baggage of anger, hate, and revenge, the bondage that is keeping me tied to my abuser. Lord Jesus, I lay it down at your feet, at the foot of the cross with your blood covering my sin, cleansing me, releasing me. I leave my abuser in your hands; he is accountable to you as I am for my sins. Thank you for the gift of truth, forgiveness and freedom. In Jesus' name, amen.*

## Stronger – Newsboys
**https://www.youtube.com/watch?v=ec6q9h_Bw6c**

# DAY 14: GOD REVEALS ONE MEMORY AT A TIME

*He reveals deep and secret things; He knows what is in the darkness, and light dwells with Him.* Daniel 2:22

God is the one who brings us to a place of revealing the pain of our past to us. I would not have faced the truth of my past without God backing me into a corner. It took being confronted with how difficult I was to live with by my daughter, or I wouldn't have faced my problems. Her words to me were, "I do not know if you are coming or going." It shook me to my core. I had repressed everything, unknowingly, to protect myself. I was a mess and did not know it. I was very confused. It was unknown to me until my symptoms were revealed.

Some of my symptoms were:

- isolation
- being defensive
- being silent
- feeling insecure
- feeling unworthy

- feeling dirty

It is difficult to be in relationship with a person who feels these things and doesn't know. It caused so much uncertainty and frustration.

**We in ourselves cannot overcome these issues alone.** Finally, after ten counselors I met a counselor who helped me see where I was and what I was doing. It all seemed so impossible. The old messages of feeling like a failure and feeling worthless had beaten me up mentally. It was one of the reasons why it took me so long to face my pain. Seeing the lies I believed released me to see myself for who I really was. It was hard to look at myself, hard to see who I was.

God said He is my lamp and He would direct my path. Knowing who God was in my pain gave me hope and courage to look at all the things I had suppressed, and to see the harm to myself and others.

*For You are my lamp, O Lord; the Lord shall enlighten my darkness. For by You I can run against a troop; by my God I can leap over a wall. As for God, His way is perfect; the word of the Lord is proven; He is a shield to all who trust in Him.* 2 Samuel 22:29-31

God did reveal to me through one memory at a time, the secret things I couldn't remember of my story. God shed the light of His word on me and I began to believe God instead of all that was untrue. **Dealing with one memory at is time is a kindness we give ourselves.** Our mind is not able to deal with more than one trauma at a time. The process of how we heal from a traumatic memory takes time to absorb, process, speak the words, acknowledge the pain, be sad, feel sorrow, and grieve over the loss. Light is truth; God shed the light of His

Word on me. I began to believe God instead of all that was untrue.

The memories come back as we acknowledge them, releasing the hold they had before. We are in a new place, and our mind is free to believe truth, not lies and there is great freedom in understanding this. There comes a time when we do not think about the pain as we once had. When you do, it will seem like a very long time ago. Releasing it again without much thought is the process of healing.

Writing my story helped me put the puzzle pieces together. I saw a picture rather than a box with a million pieces. The memories are puzzle pieces, and as I dropped them into place, I saw the picture of my life and His hand guiding me through to the next place for yet another new piece of the puzzle to be dropped into place. It is a great place to be. One puzzle piece at a time, slowly, giving time to heal and knowing God is there.

> *I will give you the treasures of darkness and hidden riches of secret places, that you may know that I, the Lord, who call you by your name, am the God of Israel.* Isaiah 45:3

God calling me by my name had deep meaning to me. I heard my name with love. He was revealing what happened to me in the dark, and it took my fear away knowing it was no longer a secret, no longer unknown. I felt God's love and tender care for me—a new experience—giving me a sense of great peace.

> *Your word is a lamp to my feet and a light to my path.* Psalm 119:105

A lamp is each step daily, and a light to my path is for the long distance journey to wholeness and a lighted path.

We cannot fix ourselves; I tried for over 60 years. **It wasn't fixing I wanted. I wanted a hedge of protection, along with safety and love, freedom and peace, and a multitude of other things stolen from me as a child. Something I never had.**

How long have you been trying to fix yourself?

Do you know what you are trying to fix or overcome?

_____
_____
_____
_____
_____
_____
_____
_____

**If you cannot answer what you are trying to fix, it could be there is nothing to fix but rather a revelation of what you need, which only God is able to supply.**

Will you allow God to reveal what you want and need to know?

What would it take to allow Him to reveal truth to you?

*Trust in Him at all times, you people; pour out your heart before Him; God is a refuge for us.* Psalm 62:8

What truth did you see today about what you believed that wasn't true?

Spend time today meditating on the above verses. What is the darkness you want light shed on?

*Father, your light sheds truth on all I believe about myself and have not known or acknowledged. I pray I have eyes to see what you are revealing, things I have not been able to see before. The pain of loss is so great. I depend on you. I pray to face the pain, sorrow over it, be sad and grieve my loss, leading me to your comfort and love. My trust is in you. I do not want to depend or defend myself any longer. In Jesus' name, I pray, amen.*

## God Help Me - Plumb
https://www.youtube.com/watch?v=Rqu7eBwhGs4

# DAY 15: HOW GOD SEES ME

*Then she (Hagar) called the name of the Lord who spoke to her, You-Are-the-God-Who-Sees; for she said, "Have I also here seen Him who sees me?"* Genesis 16:13

A few years ago, I had the privilege of meeting Jo Bailey in person. She works for Cru (formerly Campus Crusade for Christ) and was nearby in July for the bi-annual conference held in Fort Collins, on the campus of Colorado State University. We met in person after communicating by email for two years, because she heard my testimony at a church one day. It was an exciting time to meet face-to-face for the first time and share about the work we are both doing.

Jo lives in Florida, where she ministers to abused women at her church and at the county jail. As she shared her work, I found her to be vibrant, compassionate, and caring. I would like to pass along what she asks her ladies to do. At the top of a sheet of paper, write these words: "**What do You see, God, when You look at me?**"

I had been journaling for years, but had never entertained

this question. I decided to ask God the same question. It was difficult. I found myself walking all around the question before I got to the question. Justification popped up in my mind. It showed me how hard the enemy works and how my mind held onto old beliefs.

Justification was one of my walls of defense as a child and young person. It is not an easy thing to eradicate. I now recognize when I start to justify myself, and I finally ask myself, "What am I doing?" because I remember that I do not have to defend myself to God.

The Bible tells us all the ways God sees me. I started to write down what the Word of God said. Writing the words made a difference. I had to believe what I was writing. God's own words spoke volumes to my heart—they changed me.

**Accepting what God has to offer... It is a big deal.**

Will you accept who God says you are?

_____
_____
_____
_____
_____
_____
_____
_____

God says He teaches us in the way we should go. I look for His ways every day. Many are small reminders that He is just there. Sometimes they surprise me, as I notice they come at unexpected moments or places. I learn from them and write them down so as not to forget them. God is so present; He cares about me. I see who God really is; He is beautiful.

**God sees us through the lens of His love.** It is a completely different lens than the one we use to see ourselves, especially when we have suffered any kind of hurt or pain.

Write a letter to God. Tell Him how you feel and ask Him what he sees in you. What do you hear Him say to you? Praise and thank Him for what He revealed to you. Let God embrace you. You will be blessed and loved by the presence of God. Not only will He embrace you, but He will also carry you as Selah sings in the song of the day.

_____

_____

_____

_____

_____

_____

_____

_____

*And we have known and believed the love that God has for us. God is love, and he who abides in love abides in God, and God in him." 1 John 4:16*

With Jo's permission, you may view her testimony at www.JoBaileyFrazier.com

*Father, help me to see how you see me. I have a hard to time accepting how you see me. I pray for faith to trust you. Your love is*

*so big, so pure, and so beautiful. I haven't known love like this. I want your love. I pray I can fall into your arms and feel you loving me because you see me differently than I see myself. I am so glad you bring people into my life who care and ask us to write the words. 'How you see me' gives me a chance to believe you because you care about me. In Jesus name, Amen*

## I Will Carry You – Selah
https://www.youtube.com/watch?v=FlDUkpITs8A

# DAY 16: OUR THOUGHTS AFFECT OUR ACTIONS

*For where your treasure is, there your heart will be also.* Matthew 6:21

What we think about is what we treasure in our heart; it's what we believe we deserve or do not deserve. Our minds are so occupied with trying to prove our worth, we can't think about anything else. Abusive behavior toward us stunts our thoughts that we deserve anything. If we believe we do not deserve good, we will not expect good to come to us.

Have you ever thought about what you think?

Have you ever felt you deserve good things?

Abuse takes away the belief that we do not deserve anything but bad. Our ability to receive anything is lost because of this belief.

Instead, revenge and rationalization kept my mind occupied for years; it owned me. My thoughts owned me, putting me in a continuous rut that was hard to climb out of—I was stuck. I learned to cope by shutting down my damaged emotions.

> *But Jesus, knowing their thoughts, said, "Why do you think evil in your hearts?"* Matthew 9:4

Ephesians 4:31 tells us what evil is:

- Bitterness
- Wrath
- Anger
- Clamor (loud quarreling)
- Evil speaking
- Malice (wishing something bad for someone)

Keeping these things in our heart blinds us, making us believe we do not deserve any better. God created us to have value and purpose, not to please our abuser or be owned emotionally by them. Belief in these lies owns us. Even if the abuser has died, we think of them, and they are very much alive in our mind.

In our world of technology, we never are without something turned on—phones, computers, TVs, radios. Our refrigerators hum; our clocks tick. The furnace or AC is running. We hear trucks, cars, sirens—sound is everywhere.

**With all the activity around and noise going on, most of us do not think; we are just busy doing.**

I wonder, do you allow quiet to able to think?

What would happen if you did?

Would you be honest with yourself about what is going on in your heart?

_____

_____

_____

_____

_____

_____

_____

_____

*For as he thinks in his heart, so is he.* Proverbs 23:7

You form opinions by listening, by what you see, by what others are doing.

In our busy world, silence is hard to find because we are accustomed to noise and sounds coming from every direction, even without us being aware of it. We think about things with a smile on our face, but we have an empty heart. We think nothing of it or dismiss it, or do not know if what we are thinking is for our good or is for evil.

**Our thoughts define us. What is in our heart is what we think about and talk about.**

Realizing we have the wrong thoughts and wanting to change is an intentional act. It takes courage to face ourselves and realize we have empty chatter going on in our brain. It's too noisy; we are not able to think through the necessary thoughts to change our thinking. Facing the truth of the abuse, choosing to quiet the chatter of our noisy brain, and thinking through what we are thinking is the journey we travel to change the old patterns. Thinking differently takes effort on our part to overcome. It is what survivors do, or they stay the victim.

**Entering this journey is intentional; it is done with courage and tenacity. It takes guts to think truthful thoughts and speak them.** It takes time and patience, love and tears, prayer and trust in the God who gave you physical life and spiritual life through Jesus Christ. Each good thought sends good chemicals through your brain. Your brain is healing. Never say never. Do not make a vow; it will keep you from freedom.

> *Do not be deceived, God is not mocked; for whatever a man sows, that he will also reap.* Galatians 6:7

We reap what we think. Think good thoughts, right thoughts, thoughts from God's Word. Your environment will change because you are thinking differently.

What will you do to change your thought life?
Will you make a commitment to change your thought life?

___

*Father, today I come to you not knowing where to start. Forgive me for the revenge and hatred I have had in my heart. I haven't thought much about what I think about; forgive me for being so preoccupied, too busy, unaware of what is going on in my mind, my heart, and my soul. I seek you. Help me to see myself and define and recognize my thoughts. Teach me as I read your Word. I want to change my thoughts. Bring people into my life that will encourage me. Put books in my hands that are good for me. Give me eyes to see you. I want to honor you with my thought life and actions. In Your name, amen.*

**What A Wonderful Name It Is – Hillsong**
https://www.youtube.com/watch?v=nQWFzMvCfLE

# DAY 17: DON'T HURRY, TAKE TIME TO THINK

*A time to keep silence, and a time to speak.* Ecclesiastes 3:7

*Finally, my brethren, be strong in the Lord and the power of His might. Put on the whole armor of God that you may be able to stand against the wiles of the devil. Ephesian. 6:10-11*

For an abused person, taking time to think is a problem. We do not have time to think if we are running or filling every moment with busyness.

I was great at being very busy. I hurried most of the time, from one thing to another. There came a day early on in my counseling where I was asked to write a letter to my dad telling him I knew what he did, that he no longer owned me, and that his threats to me no longer bound me to secrecy. I read the letter at his grave feeling nothing, numb. I held up my torn letter, allowing it to be blown away by the wind. I left feeling empty. Not until later did a wave of peace roll over my body, my soul, and my mind. I had never felt such peace and relief in my whole life. I shall never forget the moment. **I felt as if the urgency of life had lifted from me.** It was life changing to experience, to feel a heavy weight lift off my shoulders.

When the notion to hurry comes upon me, I stop, allowing calm in my inner spirit. Relieved, the urgency to hurry dies away. I was used to having an invisible shadow chasing me into unknown hurriedness, fearing I would have to pay for being still. It is a symptom of my abuse.

The process of hurrying keeps us from having time to think. We cannot think things through or allow a time of silence. At times, we need to turn off technology—radio, television, computer, iPhones—because whatever is keeping us from having time to think, owns us.

I now love the quiet. It is peaceful. I no longer have the unknown hunting me down.

In our abuse, our minds are a mass of confusion; it was not possible to process our thoughts correctly or have clarity. We do many things to keep ourselves busy, or to keep from thinking about whose we are or where we are. Not until I knew key information about the lies of abuse was I able to put the correct information together, allowing time to think. We must be deliberate in giving ourselves a silent time to think, no matter where we are. Look at where you are; write down all the ways you excuse yourself from giving yourself time to think.

Are you able to identify what you do to not allow yourself time to think about and what you are dealing with?

Will you give yourself permission to think?

Remember, you are partnering with God as you journey on this road as a survivor. Without the strength and desire God gives, we cannot accomplish this on our own.

*Be still and know that I am God.* Psalm 46:10

The background of this verse is, "the voice of God addressing the wicked warring nations with a warning. In other words, 'Cease and desist, it is I, God, who will be exalted in victory; you do not have a chance of winning.'" (Psalm 46:10 New Spirit Filled Bible, NKJV) We cannot do this without God's help.

We are in a war with the enemy—Satan—who is trying to destroy us (John 10:10). Put on your armor (Ephesians 6:12-18); he does not want us to think through to the truth and gain victory. God will equip you to do so with the power of His Word!

Implement the sword of the Word, fight this battle thinking right thoughts, learn Scripture, express your feelings. It is possible to speak truths we did not know were possible. It gives wings to our spirit, and we want to sing and dance and embrace life like we never have before.

Isaiah 40:31 becomes real: *"but those who wait upon the Lord shall renew their strength; they shall mount up on wings of eagles, they shall run and not be weary; they shall walk and not faint."*

We are survivors. We need to think and act as a survivor to thrive. It is freedom to be who God created us to be.

I wonder who God created you to be?

Are you using "the sword of the word" to defend yourself from the onslaught of negative words you hear about yourself in your mind? (Ephesians 6:17)

Will you depend on God's word today for victory?

_____

_____

_____

_____

_____

_____

_____

You can win this battle. Know that God created you to be a warrior. Gain your territory back that the enemy stole. Seek him out; seek the truth about who God says you are in Christ Jesus.

Neil Anderson has a great book, *Victory over the Darkness*, telling you who you are in Christ Jesus. It's on my book list. Take time to read and study these great truths, because this is where your strength comes from.

*Thank you, Lord Jesus, for winning the battle to have power over death and darkness by revealing the secrets behind the lies I believe. Help me to take time to sit still, be silent thinking through things, and think right thoughts and words. You winning the victory gives me the power to overcome the confusion and lies the enemy has told me. Set me free. Give me your strength and courage to depend on your Word. Amen.*

**YouTube: Be Still My Soul – Kari Jobe**
https://www.youtube.com/watch?v=mq59iE3MhXM

# DAY 18: LISTENING WELL AND ASKING GOOD QUESTIONS

*But let your "Yes" be "Yes," and your "No" be "No." For whatever is more than these is from the evil one.* Matthew 5:37

In keeping with yesterday's reading about what we think and say, we need to be aware that our brain is healing from thinking bad thoughts when we come to this place of changing what's going on in our brain. Abuse messes with our brain in such a deceptive manner. Our mind does not mature with our body—we are immature thinkers.

*Talk no more so very proudly; let no arrogance come from your mouth, for the Lord is the God of knowledge; and by Him actions are weighed.* 1 Samuel 2:3

We can either talk too much because we cannot deal with silence or we are silent because we have nothing to say or don't know what to say. Abuse steals our capacity to know who we are. Sometimes we talk just to be talking; we do not have to be talking all the time. We do not have to give our two cents worth on every subject. Ask yourself if it is necessary to always have something to say. Don't be a know-it-all; we don't come across as well as we think. We are fooling ourselves, acting as if we have it all together.

Learning how to ask good questions is an art. A good question stimulates good conversation. We could ask, "Why do you feel strongly about what you just said?" or "How is that working for you?" By giving people the right to their opinion, we accept them for who they are. We can give our opinion and have good discussion, but it is not our business to change their mind. Our job is listening and caring about who they are.

Think about the people who provoke your mind in a good way. Why do you like being in their company? Do they bring out the best in you? Do you bring out the best in them?

_____
_____
_____
_____
_____
_____
_____
_____

Think about the person closest to you. Do you engage in only surface information or dead-end questions? Do you argue? Are you defensive? Are you contemptuous? Or do you ask, "How does it make you feel?" or "What could you do to resolve this?" Do we care what they think?

*And let us consider how we may spur one another on toward love and good works.* Hebrews 10:24 NIV

*Finally, brothers, whatever is true, whatever is noble, whatever is right, whatever is pure, whatever is lovely, whatever is admirable – if anything is excellent or praiseworthy – think about such things. Whatever you have learned or received or heard from me, put into practice. And the peace of God will be with you.* Philippians 4:8-9 NIV

Before I knew the truth about my abuse, I didn't think of these things. Now that I know the truth about the confusion of my life, I process and ask good questions. I have clarity to think things through and put things together. I am interested in what other people think, who they are, and where they come from. I value a wide range of friends who have blessed me, who provoke my mind to think, and who give me purpose other than just existing.

Are you listening well and asking good questions?

Do you know what you believe?

If so, what is the basis of what you believe?

Are your beliefs based on the Word of God? On facts? On hearsay?

Are you reading books to educate yourself; do you have the desire to stretch yourself?

Is it your desire to value another person's opinion?

Thinking rightly, speaking up, and asking good questions opens your world, grants hope, gives encouragement, values life and freedom, and provides you with a reason to get up in the morning living life with purpose and meaning. You begin to love life, love yourself, and love God.

**It is not an easy task to live as a survivor and thrive; it is done intentionally.** Remember, you are either a victim or a survivor. It is a daily commitment to seek truth, live with purpose, think well and feel good. Life is so daily. Abusive issues drag us down and putting us in the pits, scraping the walls to have air to breathe and light to see. Do not allow yourself to go back. Our thought life and how we think are key ingredients on how well we progress.

Denial, running away, not doing the work, and not facing issues keeps us from healing and overcoming. Trust God in these areas—they do not disappear because we don't want to deal with them or tell ourselves we can't. These are not options. You either move forward or regress. My prayer is that knowing this will help you "keep on keeping on" with God.

A good book to read and study is *How People Change* by Paul Tripp.

*Lord Jesus, give me right words. Please help me to process daily what I am thinking and train myself to ask good questions. I want to be a good listener, give myself grace, and not beat myself up. Help me see myself and not run from these truths, but rather face what I am doing so that I may overcome bad habits of communication. In your name I pray, amen.*

## The Lord is My Provider
https://www.youtube.com/watch?v=ZmaD6sofJMs

# DAY 19: FIRST THOUGHTS OF THE DAY

*My voice You shall hear in the morning, O Lord; in the morning I will direct it to You, and I will look up.* Psalm 5:3

What do you think about the moment you wake up in the morning? We have many demands on our life—children, food preparation, jobs, the phone ringing, car repairs, bills to be paid, urgency from every direction—too many things to do in a day for the time allotted to us. Our mind races to organize our day before our feet hit the floor.

I have discovered that my first thoughts of the day are the thoughts that direct my day. Over the years, listening to other believers and putting into practice what God leads me to do has changed my life. When I focus on God, then the demands of the day fall into place. I commit all that is on my agenda to God and ask Him for His divine appointments and direction in all that needs to be done, focusing on putting Him first and asking Him to direct my plans and making me aware of His presence.

*Give ear to my words, O Lord, consider my meditations. Give heed to the voice of my cry, my King and my God, for to You I pray.*
Psalm 5:1-2

God wants us to know, too, that we are in His thoughts and that His thoughts for us are good. Psalms 139:17 says, *"How precious also are Your thoughts to me, O God! How great is the sum of them."*

Waking up one morning, I had an unknown darkness loom over me. It wouldn't leave me. Looking in the mirror and talking to myself, I said, "This will not dictate my day, I choose not to accept the dread." This changed the mood of my day.

*I remember my affliction and wanderings, the bitterness, and the gall. I well remember them, and my soul is downcast within me. Yet this I call to mind and therefore have hope: because of the Lord's great love we are not consumed, for his compassions never fail. They are new every morning great is your faithfulness.*
Lamentations 3:19-23 NIV

The devil has his hand in the darkness and gloom. If he cannot ruin our day one way, he will try another way. Having the sword of the Word as a weapon against the darkness gives assurance that God is with me; I am not fighting the battle alone.

My attitude makes a difference when things do not go as planned. Putting God in control first makes the change. My perspective changes and I align myself to God's plan for the day.

We are not perfect. We fail; we learn. God uses these moments to conform us to the image of Christ.

*And do not be conformed to this world, but be transformed by the renewing of your mind, that you may prove what is that good and acceptable and perfect will of God.* Romans 12:2

What is your first thought in the morning when you first open your eyes?

How does it affect your mood and the productivity of your day?

_____
_____
_____
_____
_____
_____
_____
_____

The enemy wants to tangle your days and keep you from productivity. When everything goes wrong, we want to throw in the towel, and we get angry. But wait! God is allowing you to see the difference between good and evil, and he wants you to see the enemy's attack. Know that the enemy will attack with the smallest of details; allow the power of the Holy Spirit to work in your life. He is the One who gives power to overcome. Ask Him.

*Father, I commit my day to you. Help me direct my first thoughts toward you. Guide and teach me with your Word, and help me stay on track with you. I pray to learn from my failures and mistakes, doing it your way instead of mine. I want to honor you with my words and actions. In your name, amen.*

**10,000 Reason - Matt Redman**
https://www.youtube.com/watch?v=DXDGE_lRIoE

# DAY 20: HELP—I DON'T LIKE MYSELF

*O Lord, you have searched me and known me. You know my sitting down and my rising up; you understand my thought afar off. You comprehend my path and my lying down, and are acquainted with all my ways. For there is not a word on my tongue, but behold, O Lord, You know it altogether. You have hedged me behind and before, and laid Your hand upon me. Such knowledge is too wonderful for me, it is high, I cannot attain it.*
Psalm 139:1-6

'I don't like myself.' I hear this repeatedly from people who have been abused. I said it for years. I hated who I was, feeling ugly and dirty. I hated mirrors, and couldn't look myself in the eye or at the shame on my face. It couldn't be washed off—nothing could.

I felt unworthy to be loved by God. And yet, Psalm 139 tells me how much God loves and cares for me—He is pursuing me. Accepting the pursuit of God was too high for me to understand; it baffled me. I believed that Jesus died on the cross to forgive my sins, but I couldn't believe He loved me.

One day I heard Joyce Meyer say on television, "I have an

important message to tell you today— **'God. Loves. You.' Tell yourself every day, 'God loves me,' until you believe it."** It was a process, but I did it. Slowly I absorbed the truth that God loves me. I reasoned in my mind that I was slapping God in the face every time I thought about how much I hated myself while God was reaching out to love me.

*But God demonstrated His own love toward us, in that while we were yet sinners, Christ died for us.* Romans 5:8

If God loves me before I even know Him, how can I slap God in the face and insult Him by rejecting Him? He is too loving. How can I insult Him?

How can we expect anyone else to love us when we do not love ourselves or love God? We reject the very nature of God. We become arrogant and hard to live with.

Abuse is a sin against us. We, in turn, sin against others by our actions. We sin in our silence by not knowing how to answer someone or when we are unable to describe how we feel. We sin by our anger, hatred, self-protection, isolation, and moodiness. We harm ourselves with self-contempt by telling ourselves we are stupid and dumb. Coming to this realization has grieved my own soul.

I asked God to forgive me for the sin against myself. The awareness of how sinful I am as a human being is very painful, exposing my pride.

**We are unable to love because we don't believe God loves us.** Until we receive the love of God and believe, we are not able to love ourselves or anyone else. This is a part of abuse that takes time to overcome. Abuse takes away the capability to receive love, to feel lovable. We have heard many negative messages of shame, blame, unworthiness, and stupidity. Because of experiencing things like being abandoned, neglected, kicked around, beaten, locked up, or ignored, we can't accept love. Much was stolen from us. Abuse is very destructive. We must know where it comes from and who did it to realize what was stolen from us. We are fighting to get back our self-worth and dignity.

Do you hate yourself?

Can you look yourself in the eye in the mirror?

_____
_____
_____
_____
_____
_____
_____
_____

If not, hear me—God. Loves. You.

*He who does not love does not know God, for God is love.*
1 John 4:8

If you know God and you know He loves you, how can you reject His love for you? Don't slap God in the face or insult Him; accept the love He is offering you right now. Tell yourself every day, a hundred times if you must, 'God loves me,' until you believe it.

Things that have happened to you over time, and the pain you have lived with for so long will not go away in a day or two, or in a week. Your mind, body, and soul have a lot of healing to do; be kind, give yourself time to heal. Take walks, enjoy a movie, read a book, relax—all of which most abused people will not allow themselves to do. Many abused people are workaholics needing to prove their value. We run from one thing to another as fast as we can, being so driven from within. Most of the time we do not know what is driving us; we just run all the time.

If this is you, can you admit these things?

If so, what are they?

What would it take for you to change?

Take your time to process; these are hard thing to face. The truth about abuse is—it is absorbed into every fiber of your being. It is time to take care of the one person you haven't taken care of—you.

What would it look like to care for you?

_____
_____
_____
_____
_____
_____
_____
_____

Don't give up or give in. Give in to the One who loves you—God. Include a person who is close to you—a husband or a special friend, someone you know well and trust with your pain, to walk with you and encourage you.

Eliminate some things from your life to allow time to work

through these issues. It is exhausting work, and you need energy to face the new changes in your life to thrive.

*Father, looking myself in the eye is hard for me. Help me to look myself in the eye, and accept and believe how much You love me. Show me how to be kind to myself, giving myself time and space to heal. I pray, too, that you will give me energy and strength to walk on this road of healing. Amen.*

**Mirror, Mirror, on the Wall – Evie Tornquist**
https://www.youtube.com/watch?v=33_ybDK9u64

# DAY 21: ALLOWING TIME TO HEAL

*Whom will he teach knowledge? And whom will he make to understand the message? Those just weaned from milk? Those just drawn from the breast? For precept must be upon precept, precept upon precept, line upon line, line upon line, here a little, there a little.* Isaiah 28:9-10

How do you eat an elephant?

One bite at a time.

Healing from abuse is the same—one thing at a time, one layer at a time, and one day at a time.

"Life is like an onion." Start with the top layer—your current pain. It took years to build up the layers of pain, and it takes time to peel the layers off. The thin outer layer is the hardest to take off—it's telling someone that you were abused. It is coming to the place of saying, "I have been violated. I want to overcome. I want my voice."

As the layers come off, the tears start coming. Throughout my life, I cried over many things, but they were never healing tears—only tears of pain and sadness. I experienced many agonizing tears while facing my pain, dealing with it layer after layer, but they were healing tears—the best tears I ever spilled.

It takes time to process through each layer, grieve it, know the sorrow and sadness. It takes time to heal. Give yourself time to think and pray. Continue to ask God what He wants you to know. Each layer has a lie or lies attached to it; define these with words.

We are unable to bear more than one thing at a time. Identifying truth and applying it is vital in having strength for the next layer. There is always a next layer.

Even though we overcome, there are times when we must face new things; we are never done. God gives us grace to come this far; we now know how and what to do to overcome. **The gift of redemption is a daily gift. Receive it, and use it.**

An untitled poem I that have entitled "The Tapestry" (a favorite of mine for many years) also speaks to this.

> No chance hath brought this ill to me;
> 'Tis God's own hand, so let it be,
> He sees what I cannot see.
> There is a need-be for each pain,
> And He one day will make it plain
> That earthly loss is heavenly gain.
> Like a piece of tapestry
> Viewed from the back appears to be
> Naught but threads tangled hopelessly;
> But in the front a picture fair
> Rewards the worker for his care,
> Proving his skill and patience rare.
> Thou art the Workman, I the frame.
> Lord, for the glory of Thy Name,
> Perfect Thine image on the same.
> ~*Author Unknown*

One day at a time, one memory at a time, one layer at a time. It is line upon line. It is precept upon precept. Take time to sit and ponder, take time to read God's Word, and ask Him to show you the truth He wants you to know.

No matter where we are in the healing process, something often triggers our mind. Identify the trigger, ask God where the root of the memory is (where the lie lies), identify the lie, ask God for the truth about the lie in the trigger, speak the truth about this lie, and finally, speak the truth about what God says is true.

Once you identify the lie and speak the truth of it, sit in this place and grieve your loss; feel the sorrow and sadness in order to heal from this triggered pain. Give yourself time in this place to process, identify, and write the words in your journal. Weep. Say the words of truth against the lies you have believed. You must know what you are grieving and weeping for, speaking words out loud about your loss helps. Not until you know the truth and say the words will you receive release from the lies and the hold Satan has on you. This is where you overcome. When and if this issue pops up again, speak the truth out loud about the lie and speak the truth of who God says you are. It no longer has a hold on you. This is the place of victory. Use Scripture to back yourself up.

For additional help on learning this process, read Dr. Dan Allender's book, *The Wounded Heart*, chapter 10 on repentance, gives clarity on the process of shifting from holding onto pain to understanding freedom through repentance. Read it as many times as you need; make this a pattern in your healing process. You will become victorious.

Not until I grasped the depth of the trauma and the reality, could I see the necessity of dealing with and facing each pain. Only then did I gain victory. I still practice this method on a regular basis when triggered by a memory. **Redemption is**

**God's plan to work through and receive freedom.** *Your life is hidden with Christ in God.* **(Colossians 3:3)** I am safe now.

> *It is for freedom that Christ has set us free. Stand firm then, and do not let yourselves be burdened again by a yoke of bondage.*
> Galatians 5:1 NIV

God uses the hard times to strengthen us for the days ahead. We do not learn in the days of leisure, but in the days of hardship, which cannot be lived alone. We need a God who knows all things, and all things about us. Our pain is deep but God is deeper yet. He knows our heart and loves us beyond measure by teaching us about Himself.

The day will come when the darkness lies behind you, and God's glory has been revealed. As I peel back the layers of my onion, the picture of blackened harm and abuse fades into beautiful colors of liberty, grace, lovingkindness, joy, radiance, love, and a picture fair. You will become stronger and stronger in mind and body and soul. You have lived with the pain of abuse for years; give it time to fade away into joy that only comes from Jesus.

I, myself, am looking forward to that day when I will see the top side of my tapestry.

What current pain is yours today?

Can you go back to the root of that pain to see where it is coming from?

Can you identify the lie attached to it?

What is the truth God wants you to know about what you believe?

_____
_____
_____
_____
_____
_____
_____
_____

My prayers are with you in this process; trust Jesus to walk with you. Give yourself time to identify and apply this work. You may want to do this with your counselor or with a friend.

*Lord, I don't understand my pain, but you do. Teach me how to process through this memory. Show me what I believe and where it is coming from. Let me see the truth of the lie which holds me back, speak the words of truth, and live in that truth. Set me free in this place in my memory and from what I believed about myself. I pray to know the truth. Thank you for giving me eyes to see what I haven't known. I want to live in the freedom you give. Without you, I cannot overcome. I know it takes your strength to believe to set me free. In your name I pray, amen.*

**Praise You in The Storm – Casting Crowns**
https://www.youtube.com/watch?v=DoqbKyeKOBI

# DAY 22: HOW TO CARE FOR YOURSELF

*Whoever receives one little child like this in My name receives Me. But whoever causes one of these littles ones who believes in Me to sin, it would be better for him if a millstone were hung around his neck, and he were drowned in the depth of the sea.* Matthew 18:5-6

I still struggled after many years of being a believer with day-to-day victories in overcoming old patterns. As I read books on healing from abuse and talked with other women in support groups, I realized I wasn't alone. I needed their encouragement. Many victims of abuse have the same questions and frustrations regarding past issues cropping up. We need each other.

My pattern growing up was to be passive. I was not given choices; I was not allowed to make decisions or express my opinions. Children, after all, were to be seen and not heard. Consequently, I did not develop the ability to speak up for myself. I was not able to express myself. I expected my brothers to take care of me, getting rid of or fixing the problems I couldn't. I felt isolated, overlooked, and worthless.

In my years of working with others who had been abused, I saw that they shared the same feelings. We hate ourselves, sometimes unknowingly. There is too much wrong with us to feel good about ourselves. Life is difficult. We want a different life, but how to attain it is unknown.

*Therefore, if anyone is in Christ, he is a new creation; old things have passed away; behold, all things have become new.*
2 Corinthians 5:17

**God's Word tells us that when Christ is in our lives, we are a new creation. We are new! The old is gone!** We are in a new place spiritually. God is showing us around town, so to speak—showing us truth and love, showing us how to live His way. He wants us to know that we are valued—valued by Him! Think about that. Never forget God loves you! He values you!

The heart of an abused person is deeply wounded. We do not feel valued. We do not feel worthy of kindness or of anything good. We often beat ourselves up. Satan tries to keep it that way—he tries to keep us from the truth and shuts us down. He keeps us blaming ourselves and believing things about ourselves that are not true. The idea of being loved and valued is hard to imagine, but God's Word is true—it says that He loves us and cherishes us. When we believe that, we will begin caring for ourselves in the light of God's goodness and become more and more the new creation He wants us to be. The thoughts and beliefs are difficult to overcome. It takes continual work. Don't give up; sometimes it takes a while for us to get to the place of believing.

When I began writing a blog a few years ago, it gave me the mindset of processing the daily events in my life, thinking objectively about what I was doing and how I did it. It helped me to recognize the triggers that would pop me back into the old patterns, as well as the new practices that moved me forward. As you start a new chapter in your life of actively seeking healing and learning to care for yourself, here are some very practical things that I learned and want to pass on to you:

- Go to bed at a regular time and get enough rest.
- Go for a 20-30 minute walk every day.
- Drink half your weight in ounces of water every day.
- Ask one or two people to pray for you while you are in this healing process.
- Eliminate some of your extra activities. You need time to think through and process what you are learning.

**These are not frivolous things. It is important to take time for yourself while you are healing, to give yourself margin in your day of work.** Caring for yourself—being kind to yourself—may be new to you. If you don't care for yourself, who will? If you struggle with caring for yourself, ask the Lord to help you. You might pray something like this: "Father, today I want to take care of myself. Help me to schedule time to take a walk and breathe deeply to regain peace, to rest in your truths, to believe you love me. Help me believe that I am valuable to you. Thank you for showing me where to start. Amen."

Sit and soak in the truths you have learned: God loves you and values you. *If anyone is in Christ, he is a new creation; old things have passed away; behold, all things have become new* (2 Corinthians 5:17). In Christ, you are now a new creation! My prayer for you is that you will picture yourself in God's loving presence, know you are valued, and treat yourself to at least one kindness each day.

What is your act of kindness to yourself today?

_____
_____
_____
_____
_____
_____
_____
_____

*Father, I have recognized how seductive Satan is in my life, believing lies that are not true. I haven't taken good care of myself or given myself margin in my day to think and process what I am thinking. I do hate myself. Help me recognize that is not how you see me. I am a new creature, old things have passed away, and I am in a new place. I will allow myself to rest, be kind, and value myself. In Jesus' name, amen.*

**God Will Take Care of You**
https://www.youtube.com/watch?v=MdZ7RdFo7Eo

# DAY 23: BOUNDARIES

*It is for freedom that Christ has set us free. Stand firm, then, and do not let yourselves be burdened again by a yoke of slavery.*
Galatians 5:1 NIV

Boundaries are developed when we realize who we are in Christ Jesus. We can only feel safe when we know the truth about who we are, have a voice, and express our own feelings, emotions and ideas. Before we knew we are in Christ Jesus, we doubted ourselves, our decisions, and our value of existence. Abuse steals those things from us. Abuse robs us of our God-given qualities; it shuts down our personality. It cripples our ability to do what we were intended to do. We become grounded when we know who we are in Christ Jesus.

**The question we must ask ourselves is: do I want to be living free?**

Neil Anderson explains who we are in Christ in his book *Victory over the Darkness*. All of this is contrary to what we believe about ourselves when we come from any kind of abuse. Unless we believe who Jesus says we are in Him, we will not have the confidence to stand in the truths of the Word of God. Our identity in Christ gives us strength and courage to stand for what we believe about God and ourselves. We must know these truths.

**Unless we depend on and live like we are valuable, we will not have boundaries.** Coming from a background of abuse, we are unaware we have choices, we are manipulated, we have no voice in what we think and do, we can't express our opinion, and we back down on every issue. We have the option of saying "no," of living with the knowledge of who we are. Being in Christ changes everything. Everything God designed you to have from the day you were born—His image and the plans He has for you—were stolen from you through the abuse. Abuse robs us of our God-given qualities. It shuts down our personality and it cripples our ability—what God intended for us to do and be— forcing us to live a life of fear, shame, insecurity, and a sense of guilt of something always being wrong with us.

You may say, "I pray."

What are you praying for?

Truth?

Freedom?

Safety?

Prayer without action will get you nowhere. God has a part and we have a part. Talk to a safe person—a teacher, a trusted friend, a counselor. Read books related to your issue. Memorize key verses related to your situation; use God's Word when you need encouragement. Unless you act, nothing will happen. Do your part of speaking up; you have a choice. Look for people who can help you. You must do the work. You must believe. You must act.

Depending on someone else to do your work will not gain you the freedom or truth you desire; it must come from your heart. Experiencing the Word of God, practicing the truth, and seeking the unknown are all a part of growing up emotionally. You must establish fortitude to gain the ability to overcome the pain.

Boundaries do not happen overnight; it is a process like everything else. We practice having a voice once we have admitted we need help, sought out the people who can help, identified the pain, spoken the words of truth, becoming grounded in who we are in Christ as a human being. This is freedom from the tight controls we have lived under because of the abuse or harm we have endured. It is living outside of the grip of fear and shame.

**Victims do not know they have no boundaries; they are made to believe they have no choices. Our choices are owned by the abuser. Abusers know their victims well, better than they know themselves.** They are keen on observing you before they choose you as a victim, in order to know your frailties. They meet you where your needs are and treat you well. Once you are in their grip, their personality changes to that of a predator, and they twist the truth to make you believe you are the one creating this stranglehold. They blame you for what they are doing.

You, as a victim, do not know you can say "no." Each abuser is different, and each case of abuse is different. However, the belief system of an abuse victim is crippled, and our foundation is built on their lies and cruelty to our spirit. It is what we believe about ourselves that is hard to heal from once we are away from our abuser.

Even being away from them, or living miles apart, they still own our spirit because we are unaware of the hold they have on our minds. We have learned to defend ourselves; our defense mechanism is what holds us captive. We are still operating as a victim because we do not know the truth of how they have controlled us. Unless that control is broken by our deliberate, intentional desire to be set free from our pain of what they did—facing the facts—they will continue to have a hold on us, even if they have passed away.

We develop in these areas slowly, breaking the hold of old patterns. Change does not occur overnight. Your desire to overcome comes with hope and courage; facing the fears and shame will be what sets you free.

"The only identity equation that works in God's kingdom is you plus Christ equals wholeness and meaning." ~Neil Anderson (*Victory over the Darkness,* page 27.)

I have not met anyone who has overcome the effects of abuse unless Jesus Christ is in the center of their life. There is not enough strength or courage we can muster up to continuing to live as a survivor without the power of Christ in us. We cannot forgive without the love of God to overcome the intense anger, hatred, revenge, or whatever else you are holding on to. I certainly never could, and I tried for over sixty years.

Our minds are very good at trying to live in independence from God. We may think we can, but in the end, we are the greatest fool.

*Come to me, all you who are weary and burdened, and I will give you rest. Take my yoke upon you and learn from Me, for I am gentle and humble in heart, and you will find rest for your souls. For my yoke is easy and My burden is light.* Matthew 11:28-30 NIV

Every area of our healing process stems from the same belief—that we are worthless and unlovable. We do not believe in ourselves. Every person has one major lie they believe that is difficult to overcome. Satan will milk that belief for all it's worth to keep you from thriving.

*Father, I am tired and weary from trying so hard to be set free. I run and I fight, but it has not worked. I come to you, and I lay down my pain. Show me the truth of the lies I believe. Let me know where I can set the boundaries I need to be safe and learn*

*what I need to know to protect myself with your truths of who I am in You. Give me clarity to see who I am and live freely. I pray to stand firm in You, amen.*

## My Hope is Built on Nothing Less – Norton Hall Band
https://www.youtube.com/watch?v=EVE-xXFDOwg

# DAY 24: TRUST

*Trust in the Lord with all your heart, and lean not on your own understanding.* Proverbs 3:5-6

Not long ago, a person who was abused asked me, "How do you trust again?" I searched a long time for that answer. My answer is—there is no simple answer. It's a process.

To trust again has been a long journey for me. Everybody's story is different, but the symptoms of abuse follow a very similar pattern.

For most of my life, I didn't know that I didn't trust. I had been very passive, doing what other people said. As a small child, I didn't speak much. I had been told many times "Children are to be seen and not heard," and as a result I didn't question much. I did not have the vocabulary to express my feelings. I just accepted what was said and did it. When you aren't allowed to speak, you do not develop a vocabulary.

While I was in counseling again at age sixty-one, the process of answering questions revealed my lack of trust. I defended myself and had wrong motives. I was angry and afraid of being blamed and criticized, both of which made me fearful of what anyone thought of me. My trust for God was very vague. Why didn't I trust? Not having a foundation of trust in childhood from a trustworthy person shatters the ability to trust anyone, and life is unstable. The revelation of my not trusting was wrapped up in my feeling unworthy; I did not feel worthy to be loved. It is a vicious cycle and shuts me down.

I have known Romans 5:8 for a very long time: *But God demonstrates His own love toward us, in that while we were still sinners, Christ died for us.* I knew and loved that verse, but I looked at it as if it were for somebody else or for the corporate body—for everybody but me. I didn't understand how or why God loved *me*. I didn't understand how to accept what God had to offer. But the verse would not let me go. All I knew was I did not like myself, so why would God love me? I did not know where it came from. It was a hard process, and I hated it. It wore me out to even think of it. The question had answers, but I didn't want to answer. I couldn't say the words.

I had a hard time accepting the fact that the symptoms of the abuse were linked to the abuse. My mind couldn't fathom that a person of trust could abuse a child. It overwhelmed me. When it finally sunk in, I wanted to scream. I couldn't. I had learned well to suppress my terror and pain, and I couldn't scream. The frustration put anger on top of anger.

In my childhood, being angry was another thing that wasn't allowed. I was finally coming to grips with all the pain I had carried by denying my feelings and suppressing my anger for so many years. It found out that it was healthy to be angry about what happened; this is justified anger. We have to be angry to persevere.

All these questions and discoveries were the process of facing and dealing with all that had been penned up inside of me for over sixty years. It was a time of healing. I was learning where the pain came from. It was not from anything I did, but from the harm that was done to me. I had lost many things, and trust was one of them.

> *Who is among you who (reverently) fears the Lord, who obeys the voice of His Servant, yet who walks in darkness and deep trouble and has no shining splendor (in his heart)? Let him rely on, trust in, and be confident in the name of the Lord, and let him lean upon and be supported by God.* Isaiah 50:10 AMP

Trust doesn't come overnight. Be still. Sit and ponder God's love and grace. Give yourself time to see God in your heart and mind and enjoy the peace that comes with God's presence. Talk to God, and give Him your uncertainty.

**Just because we are believers, doesn't mean we do not have doubts, fears, and uncertainty. We must learn to overcome by facing it, dealing with it, confessing it and asking questions.** And we also relearn because we forget or become familiar with something.

> *(So that we might be) to the praise and the commendation of His glorious grace (favor and mercy), which He so freely bestowed on us in the Beloved. In Him we have redemption (deliverance and salvation) through His blood, the remission (forgiveness) of our offenses (shortcomings and trespasses), in accordance with the riches and the generosity of His gracious favor. Which He lavished upon us in every kind of wisdom and understanding (practical insight and prudence), making known to us the mystery (secret) of His will (of His plan, of His purpose). (And this is it) In accordance with His good pleasure (His merciful intention) which He had previously purposed and set forth in Him.* Ephesians 1:6-9 AMP

What powerful words! What a wonderful gift this is to us who have never been loved like this before! God loves us lavishly. Be kind to yourself; trust in the Lord one day at a time. You will find that God is there for you. Look for him in the details of your life. Read this portion of Scripture; in mediating on it, you will see and meet God. Find other verses that speak to you, and park on them for a time. Read the cross reference, soak them in, and absorb them. Write them down, reread them, own them. Trust will grow and be yours.

*Blessed be God, who has not turned away from my prayer, nor His mercy from me.* Psalm 66:20

I love God; He never fails me.

**If you have a time you think He is failing you, then wait. He is working out the details to give you His favor at the right time.**

*Father, thank you for encouraging me to trust you today. I am in a hurry to know that you are there, but give me the patience to wait on your timing to do the things I need in my life to trust you. Give me eyes to see you in my daily walk with you as I wait upon you and trust you little by little, day by day. I praise you for all you have revealed to my heart today. In your beautiful Name I pray, amen.*

**I've Been Through Enough – C.T. and Becky Townsend**
https://www.youtube.com/watch?v=bnLilmNClgM

## DAY 25: KINDNESS

*And be kind to one another, tenderhearted, forgiving one another, even as God in Christ forgave you.* Ephesians 4:32

Coming from an abusive background, we know little of kindness, either from others or toward ourselves. Kindness is very foreign to us. Kindness from abusive people is used for manipulations. When we do not respond or are not performing, it turns into threats and ugliness. We pay for not performing. There is no trusting kindness when it is used against us. Therefore, we cannot or will not believe kindness is good or exists.

Because of the abuse we do not feel we deserve kindness. We are constantly belittling ourselves, putting ourselves down, condemning ourselves with phrases such as, "I am so stupid, an idiot, a klutz. I never get anything right. I hate myself. I am no good. Who would want me?"

Self-contempt owns us, and we do not know the extent of the damage. We are accustomed to speaking negative self-talk to ourselves, and we don't realize we are doing it. We have heard negative talk for so long that we do not believe in ourselves. Speaking negative words is a self-fulfilling prophecy. Changing self-talk takes time and effort. It changes things.

What does it look like to stop the negative self-talk and show ourselves kindness? It is not a small thing. It takes time to see ourselves as Jesus sees us—without blemish. It seems impossible, but it is possible.

Do you recognize the self-contempt you carry for yourself?

_____
_____
_____
_____
_____
_____
_____
_____

Ask God to help you find new words to speak of yourself. It will not change overnight, but as you practice, you will begin to see changes in how you feel about yourself. You will become less self-condemning. A word search in the Bible on "kindness" gives a new perspective on the topic.

*Or do you show contempt for the riches of his **kindness**, forbearance and patience, not realizing that God's **kindness** is intended to lead you to repentance?* Romans 2:14

*The Lord appeared to us in the past, saying: "I have loved you with* *an everlasting love; I have drawn you with unfailing **kindness**.* Jeremiah 31:3 NIV

*Beloved, let us love one another, for love is of God; and everyone who loves is born of God and knows God.* 1 John 4:7

We can believe God loves us and leave self-contempt behind.

Will you have ears to hear that God calls you "Beloved?"

Will you embrace the God who loves you?

What new words will you say to yourself to break the habit of unkindness and self-condemning words?

**God is the essence of love. He is waiting for you to run into His waiting arms so He can show you His loving kindness today and every day.**

*At one time we too were foolish, disobedient, deceived and enslaved by all kinds of passions and pleasures. We lived in malice and envy, being hated and hating one another. But when the kindness and love of God our Savior appeared, he saved us, not*

> *because of righteous things we had done, but because of his mercy. He saved us through the washing of rebirth and renewal by the Holy Spirit, whom he poured out on us generously through Jesus Christ our Savior, so that, having been justified by his grace, we might become heirs having the hope of eternal life. This is a trustworthy saying. And I want you to stress these things, so that those who have trusted in God may be careful to devote themselves to doing what is good. These things are excellent and profitable for everyone.* Titus 3:3-8 NIV

Because of all that God has provided for us, we can let go of unkindness and self-contempt. Embrace who God created you to be, and all He has given you. Acceptance—a gift of kindness for yourself—is life changing. It is a new place to live, and a place of new beginnings. God's kindness is so beautiful, pleasant, and peaceable.

> *We will rejoice in your salvation, and in the name of our God we will set up our banners! May the Lord fulfill all your petitions.* Psalm 20:5

Personalizing this verse can give deep meaning for you.

Kindness from others is demonstrated in many ways: through thoughtful acts, eyes that speak love, a helping hand, and trust and confidence in your abilities when you think you can't do things. It is a kindness for you to accept what others offer.

Will you allow yourself to receive kindness?

_____
_____
_____
_____
_____
_____
_____
_____

*Father, kindness is hard for me to accept. Help me stop the old messages. I will speak kind words, not speaking self-condemning talk. I pray defensiveness, self-condemnation and unkindness will dissolve by believing you love me. Help me speak words of truth about who you say I am—Your beloved. In your Name I pray, amen.*

### Cornerstone – Hillsong
https://www.youtube.com/watch?v=izrk-erhDdk

# DAY 26: STAND FIRM AGAINST THE ENEMY

*For I know the thoughts that I think toward you, says the Lord, thoughts of peace and not of evil, to give you a future and a hope. Then you will call upon me and go and pray to me, and I will listen to you. And you will seek Me and find Me, when you search for me with all your heart. I will be found by you, says the Lord, and bring you back from your captivity; I will gather you from all the nations and from the places from which I cause you to be carried away captive.* Jeremiah 29:11-14

When I finished counseling, I kept saying to myself, "I'm done." Little did I know, it was just the beginning of healing and new life. Having lived as a victim for over sixty years, I did not know who I was or how to live as a survivor. I was starting over.

I said to the Lord, "I feel like a spider hanging on a web, dangling midway between the ceiling and the floor. I am going to crash and burn." In my spirit, I heard God's voice say to me, "You've got Me." Those three words gave me so much hope.

I asked myself these questions: "What does it look like to start over? Where do I start? Who am I? What do I think?

Where do I go? What do I say? How do I respond?" Everything was different.

Not knowing any of the answers to these questions, I sat. I sat before the Lord, numb, blank, and wondering. I did only what I had to. Looking back, it was the best place to be. I was in that state for six months. In this state, God was healing me in ways I cannot tell you or explain. All I know is God was there, and I knew it. I sensed His presence and He was healing me. He healed my heart and mind. At the end of the year, I felt totally different emotionally, and I was excited about life like never before.

Life was worth living. I experienced a different frame of mind, depending on the Lord, being curious, started asking questions. I stopped second guessing, began listening and learning, and started having confidence.

Isaiah 61 speaks of all that God has done for me: *The spirit of the Lord is upon me, and he has anointed me.* He gave me freedom from the captivity of all the lies I had believed, and I was able to come out of my own prison of fear and shame. God has given me comfort when I have mourned my losses—beauty for ashes, the oil of joy for mourning, a garment of praise for a spirit of heaviness. He has given me righteousness, that He might be glorified. He has rebuilt the old ruins, raised up from the former desolations, and repaired the ruins.

Instead of shame, He has given me double honor. Instead of confusion I rejoice, and I possess double—I have my life back and I have freedom. Everlasting joy is mine, because the Lord loves justice. I am greatly rejoicing because Jesus has given me a garment of salvation and a robe of righteousness.

Do you have a time and place when you were released from your prison? Date it, if you can.

If so, what did it look like?

Knowing these things puts you in a new place. We can speak against the enemy when he comes to us in unsuspecting times in our lives—at night when you wake up and fear grips you, or when you are forcing a quick decision. We can say "no" to Satan when he attacks us. Satan will attack you. He wants you to fail; do not give him the privilege of throwing you back into the pit. Stand firm. (Ephesians 6:12)

We must know how the enemy works to be able to stand against him. He blindsides us and keeps us busy with undone things. You will have relational issues; things will go wrong. Remember: *These things I have spoken to you, that in Me you may have peace. In the world you will have tribulation: but be of good cheer, I have overcome the world.* John 16:33

We are in warfare against the unseen enemy of this world. He is out to get you and you must know his schemes to fight back. To think like an overcomer, you must be an overcomer. It is hard work, and we should be aware that opposition will come, preparing for the spiritual warfare.

**Do not worry about pleasing other people. Other people's expectations are not our responsibility.** You cannot please man and God at the same time. You will either love one or hate the other or you will be on the fence.

*No one can serve two masters; for either he will hate the one and love the other, or else he will be loyal to the one and despise the other.* Matthew 6:24 NIV

The entry on February twelfth in Mrs. Charles E. Cowman's devotional book, *Streams in the Desert*, includes a quote by Arthur Christopher Bacon: "I can still believe that a day comes for all of us, however far off it may be, when we shall understand; when these tragedies that now blacken and darken the very air of heaven for us, will sink into their places in a scheme so august, so magnificent, so joyful, that we shall laugh for wonder and delight."\*

**Only God can use something bad and turn it into something good.** Distressing events happen every day to people everywhere. God uses the things of this world to reveal Himself and let us know we can't handle them without Him. It is how we come to know this mighty God who loves us.

*Lord Jesus, because of your Word I can stand firm against the enemy. You give me strength, power and might in the presence of harm from the enemy. "You are my strength and shield and in you I will trust."Psalm 28:7. You are my provider of eternal things. You set me free from every stronghold because I have words to speak against the enemy. Jesus is here with me in time of my need. You know my trials because you suffered them too. Thank you, Jesus. I love what you have done for me. Amen.*

**God is My Refuge – Dudley Smith**
https://www.youtube.com/watch?v=Nkr7H6AXl3I

# DAY 27: LAUGH AGAIN

*Then our mouth was filled with laughter, and our tongue with singing.* Psalm 126:2

In the very first recovery class I led, I asked, "Do you know how to have fun?" Of the six people in the class, every one of them said they had a difficult time having fun. Abused people have a problem relaxing or having a good time. Most of us do not know how to play. I have found this to be a problem not just for me and my first class, but for every subsequent class as well.

I was programmed to work and produce so as not waste time. I became hyper-vigilant at second guessing people and situations, which made me very tense.

**Abuse restricts our ability to relax.** It's difficult to sit still and enjoy a leisurely conversation, or to do anything in a relaxed manner. I observed how I ate fast, drank in gulps instead of sips, and jumped up thinking I had to do everything. I hated what I had become, and learning to relax has taken time and effort.

I wonder, have you had similar experiences?

Dr. Caroline Leaf, a brain physician and scientist, has several books out on how the brain works. *Who Switched Off My Brain? Controlling Toxic Thoughts and Emotions* helped me understand that trauma created holes in the brain, causing the inability to remember things. *Who Switched On My Brain? The Key to Peak Happiness, Thinking, and Health* is filled with scripture to validate truth and all Jesus did for us. Both books are very encouraging. They teach us to know that our brain can heal by changing our thought life, which sends healthy chemicals into our brain to rebuild and repair the holes in our brain.

Dr. Leaf's books also helped me understand how intricately God has made us, giving us insight into where we are coming from.

**Laughter is good for us, learn to laugh.** Chuck Swindoll reminded me of this on his radio program when he recommended listening to Art Linkletter's old television series "Kids Say the Darndest Things." It's guaranteed you to make you laugh. Dr. Swindoll says if you cannot laugh at that, there is something wrong with you.

*Finally, brothers, whatever things are true, whatever things are noble, whatever things are just, whatever things are pure, whatever things are lovely, whatever things are of good report, if there is any virtue and if there is anything praiseworthy— meditate on these things.* Philippians 4:8

*He will yet fill your mouth with laughing and your lips with rejoicing.* Job 8:21

Laughing and learning how to play are good for us. We

need these times to reboot our lives. Give yourself time to play and to laugh. Invite a friend to enjoy a leisurely lunch. Have fun.

How will you make plans to relax?

Rent a comedy movie?

___

Don't jump up every time something needs to be done. Do yourself a favor: sit back and watch the dynamic of the family. Find humor in reactions and make light of them instead of being tense. Give yourself permission to ask someone to do something for you, and enjoy the pleasure of being waited on. Smile more often. Breathe. It is all a part of relaxing to laugh again.

> *Father, I want to be able to relax and enjoy friends, playing, and laughing. I give myself permission to relax, letting go of old messages to perform, and growing in this area where I wasn't allowed to or given to opportunity to. The thought of it makes me happy. I am glad you have exposed this hyper-vigilance in me. Thank you, Jesus. Amen.*

**Laughter in the Rain – Neil Sedaka**
https://www.youtube.com/watch?v=VCusyLPrFCo

# DAY 28: ASK GOD HOW TO LOVE

*And now abide faith, hope, and love, these three; but the greatest of these is love.* 1 Corinthians 13:13

Back at age twenty-five, I had a great friend take me under her wing. I was struggling in my marriage and being a new mom for the second time. One day she said to me, "Ask God to teach you how to love."

I was not in a good place at this time because of memories of having to do mundane things for my dad, who did nothing for himself. All the family was at his beck and call day and night. I resented doing anything for anybody that was capable of doing things for themselves. I had so much resentment that I had a hard time doing anything for my husband.

Those words threw me. What did she mean? She said to ask God to help me do one thing a day to show love the way God wanted me to love him. I was in a desperate place. I had no idea how to love like that. Not having seen love demonstrated, I did not know how to care for and love him. It seemed like a simple thing, but it was hard work for me to break my old pattern of thinking—and hating—to do something for an able-bodied person.

God used that simple task to teach me to love with His love. I was not capable of loving with my love. I realized my love was only for selfish gain, not for what I could give. Only God's love within me could help me love my husband with God's love. It was a process that changed my heart and our marriage. I saw my husband with new eyes.

As new believer in Jesus, I did not know much about what Jesus meant in the Bible. I took baby steps in reading the Bible, in praying and in acting out what God said to do. I gradually began to think and ask God for help in the daily tasks of just living out what I was learning from the Bible. Slowly, my heart began to change.

I remember looking back six months later after asking God to show me how to love and seeing that there were changes I had never before experienced or seen before in my life at this point. I was excited. God cared that much about me, teaching me a new and different way with His love.

*So, I say to you, ask, and it will be given to you; seek, and you will find; knock, and it will be opened to you.* Luke 11:9

God tells us to ask, seek, knock, and we shall find. He gives what we need when we ask.

*Greater love has no man than this, than to lay down one's life for his friends.* John 15:13

I had to lay down my wrong thinking about how I loved.

*Call on Me, and I will answer you, and I will show you great and mighty things, which you do not know.* Jeremiah 33:3

I used this verse for many of my challenges. God has been so good to me. It was a slow process and a challenge because my heart was so calloused toward trust. Slowly, sometimes painstakingly, things changed as I sought God and all He had to offer. I found Him to be faithful, kind, and gracious to me.

**God is calling us to love. Unless we know who He is and how much He loves us, we will not understand love. Love is the essence of God. His very being is love.** Until we receive Him, we cannot fathom love. Love to me is still bigger than we can comprehend; it is truly the most beautiful gift we can receive.

My prayer for you is to accept the love of God and embrace it. Embrace it for today and tomorrow. Embrace it again and again and again. Everyday embrace it until you feel you are loved by God. It is how God taught me to love.

My heart goes to a song I learned growing up—*My Faith Looks Up to Thee,* by Ray Palmer:

> *My faith looks up to thee, Thou Lamb of Calvary,*
> *Savior divine!*
> *Now hear me while I pray, take all my guilt away,*
> *O let me from this day be wholly thine.*
> *May Thy rich grace impart, strength to my fainting*
> *heart, my zeal inspire;*
> *As Thou hast died for me, O may my love to thee,*
> *pure, warm and changeless be, a living fire.*
> *While life's dark maze I tread and griefs around me*
> *spread, be Thou my guide;*
> *Bid darkness turn to day, wipe sorrow's tears away,*
> *nor let me ever stray from Thee aside.*
> *When ends life's passing dream, when death's cold*
> *threatening stream shall over me roll,*

> *Blest Savior, then, in love, fear and distrust remove;*
> *O lift me safe above, a ransomed soul.*

We may never know where the person who harmed us came from, their background, their past pain, or why they choose to hurt us. They might have thought it would relieve their pain, when it only made it worse for themselves. They stole our capacity to love. Because of their harm, we are not capable of loving unless we seek to change our actions. We must want to reclaim ourselves and do the hard work of speaking the truth of our abuse for God to give to back to us all the beauty we had before these things happened.

Love is a learned process. Ask God to teach you how to love. On our part, loving well depends on our part of accepting love, and choosing to receive it. Once we accept and receive love we can love others. Loving ourselves is hard for an abused person, but understanding who God is and His essence of love begins the process of learning to love ourselves. This is a key component of loving others.

Love changes our perspective of our brokenness and pain. God reveals Himself in our pain. We can see new life emerging in our hearts as we turn our face to the light of God's love, walk in it, and experience it.

> *Heavenly Father, love is hard for me. I have not seen this kind of love. My heart has been broken and wounded. Give my eyes a fresh new perspective on what love looks like. Help me daily to love by doing a simple thing I haven't been willing to do. Make me willing. Soften my spirit within to accept love. Amen.*

Music is a great way to give a melody to our heart, and it helps us remember. Here is another song to encourage you:

**Love Broke Thru – TobyMac**
https://www.youtube.com/watch?v=44l9PRI4c2M

## DAY 29: RESTING IN GOD

*And He said, "My Presence will go with you, and I will give you rest. Exodus 33:14*

Did you ever wonder what it means to rest in God? Are you supposed to be still, lying down, sitting, or doing nothing? I satisfied my curiosity by reading every verse on "rest" in the concordance of my Amplified Bible years back. I dated the verses and found my journal to refresh my mind about what I learned about rest. I did the study over a period of five months in order to ponder, process, and practice what God was teaching me from each verse and corresponding verses.

God's presence did go with me as I soaked in Scripture.

*You made known to them Your holy Sabbath, and commanded them precepts, statues, and laws, by the hand of Moses Your servant. You gave them bread from heaven for their hunger, you brought them water out of the rock for their thirst, and you told then to go in and possess the land which You had sworn to give them. Nehemiah 9:14-15*

God did this for me. I read His Word, I soaked it in, and I drank deeply all He said to do. I have possessed the rest He offered which He said I would have. There is more than one kind of rest. Not only does He give rest in our soul during busyness but He also gives rest on the Sabbath. Not everyone can rest on the same day. Our bodies were made to rest one day a week, no matter what designated day we rest. With all the variety of jobs and lifestyles, we cannot all rest on the same day. Do not feel guilty; find a day to rest your body, mind, and soul.

In my journal on August 15, 2005, I wrote: **"Rest is not a place to sit down or a result of sleep, but a place God takes us when we are living in obedience to Him. A place of knowing who He is, what He does and has done. It is quiet place in the heart of dependence on Him for every moment no matter what is going on."** A well-learned lesson on my state of "being."

*The Rest of God,* written by Mark Buchanan, says, "God's solution is surprising. He offers rest. But it's a unique form of rest. It is to rest in him during our trials and our burdens. It is discovering, as David did in seasons of distress, that God is our rock and refuge right in the thick of our situation."

I read this book before I found out the truth of all my symptoms of abuse. I learned I needed to place my rest in God during that difficult time. God was so gracious to teach me so much about Himself and build me up before I came to this distressing place in life.

*For the Lord is good; His mercy is everlasting, and His truth endures to all generations.* Psalms 100:5

Do you seek rest from the distresses in your life?
Will you seek to know the rest God is offering you?

What is your plan of action to find rest in God?

_____
_____
_____
_____
_____
_____
_____
_____

*Father, you gave your Word to show me what I need, how to do it, and the results of my actions. I give you my time to spend quiet moments seeking you. I will write down what you teach me, knowing I will forget if I don't. Give me a hungry heart and a thirsty soul that I may possess the promises you have offered to me. I want to find the place of rest and dependency on you to enter the rest you have for me. Amen.*

**There is a Quiet Place – Heritage Singers**
https://www.youtube.com/watch?v=6AUz9bXwvb8

# DAY 30: PRACTICE, PRACTICE, PRACTICE

*The thief does not come except to steal, and to kill, and to destroy. I have come that they may have life, and that they may have it abundantly.* John 10:10

Every victim of sexual abuse goes through loss in how they think and feel about themselves. There is so much pain in the world; many people are suffering from one kind of abuse or another. After we learn the truth and can identify some of the things we feel and believe, the enemy, Satan, will do everything in his power to get us back to the place of living like a victim again. He'll aim to get you to lose the grip of truth and begin to believe the lies again, to keep you from living a victorious life in Christ Jesus. Unless you build a relationship with Jesus daily, you will once again be sucked into being a victim. Remember—Satan wants to destroy you.

We as survivors need daily encouragement from God's Word to gain the victory in the events that surprise us—triggers, words you hear other people say, sounds, little idiosyncrasies. You will hear things you would never have thought of, and they will throw you into a crazy cycle of, "What's wrong with me?" and "Where did that come from?"

What does it take to overcome?

What will keep me on the right path?

_____
_____
_____
_____
_____
_____
_____
_____

I have found that having a daily appointment with God, knowing who He is and all He has provided, builds me up and gives me courage to keep on keeping on. We all go through this process, though we have the same questions with different words.

**We need to know it's okay to be where we are. Practice what you learn and read God's Word. Put it to work; prove it.**

*Whatever you have learned or received or heard from me – put into practice. And the God of peace will be with you.* Philippians 4:9 NIV

*Your word is a lamp to my feet (each step) and a light to my path (long range).* Psalm 119:105

*If we say that we have fellowship with Him, and walk in darkness, we lie and do not <u>practice</u> the truth.* 1 John 1:6

**Every thought is a choice; practice every choice.** It is mental work, and it takes time. Be deliberate, believing God for everything. Train yourself to think right. If negative thoughts come to our mind or something bad pops up, tell yourself, "I am not going there." Talk to yourself, repeat Scripture relating to your issue, and find yourself saying it multiple times. You are fighting the good fight of spiritual warfare.

*Fight the good fight of faith, lay hold on eternal life, to which you were also called and have confessed the good confession in the presence of many witnesses.* 1 Timothy 6:12

You will see progress as you practice everything. We as survivors can never let down our guard. We must prevail and become strong as well as encouraging others.

*Father, I fail so many times because I forget to use the tools you have provided for me. Provoke me to remember to practice the things you reveal. Your promises assure me you are with me in the tough times—give me remembrance of the words to use if I forget. Give me courage to face the things that seem easy but are hard to do. I need you. Amen.*

**The More I seek You - Kari Jobe**
https://www.youtube.com/watch?v=b4crRPpqoW4

## DAY 31: FORGIVENESS

*But He was wounded for our transgressions, He was bruised for our iniquities; the chastisement for our peace was upon Him, and by His stripes we are healed. Isaiah 53:5*

Forgiveness has been one of the most challenging things I have faced in the whole process of healing. For most of my life, I hung on to revenge, and I wanted a payback, even though I did not know from what or for what. Because my abuse was buried so deep in my subconscious mind I did not remember the actual abuse but lived with so many of the symptoms. I wanted something; I just did not know what it was.

Someone had to pay, but for what? I wanted something. I could not put my finger on it; money or things would not satisfy. Not until I came through counseling and was in a Journey group did I have words for what I wanted: My life was stolen from me and I wanted it back.

When abuse occurs, the abusive person owns you. They own you because your mind will not let go of the hate, anger, revenge, or whatever else holds you to them. I rehearsed words over and over in my mind, words that spewed out all that venom, and I wanted answers; but no answers came. It was a mind game, a mental movie that played over and over in my mind thousands of times, yet I never won. I was in a deep rut of pain and agony wanting revenge—a pay back.

In spite of all my years of Bible study, reading books, seminars, the truth, love and all God had to offer, forgiveness came together slowly in that area. The process started slowly while I was in counseling when I saw all Jesus did in His coming, His life, His purpose, and His plan of redemption. How deep was His loss and sacrifice for my sins! How much was he hated, accused, and blamed for nothing He ever did, but for all that I did (and all we as sinners have done)! He paid for the penalty of all our sins.

He did not defend Himself, He was silent, and He never spoke a word. He willingly died so we could have forgiveness. The reality of all He did became so real for me, I ached for the pain He endured and didn't deserve on that cross. He knew my pain and willingly carried it to the cross and shed His blood for me. If He loved me that much, surely, I could forgive all my losses and pain. I began to see the pain in my dad's life. I pieced together stories I had heard, what I knew, and my conclusion was that his pain was great, too. I was not giving him a reason for what he did, but rather understanding what kind of life he must have had and didn't have. The harm he suffered gave me a new picture of him. I put on my "Jesus glasses" and saw his side of life. It was very, very sad. I understood things I hadn't understood, and it gave me the ability to let go of the revenge and hate, and forgive.

> *And forgive us our debts as we forgive our debtors... For if you forgive men their trespasses, your Heavenly Father will also*

*forgive you. But if you do not forgive men their trespasses, neither will your Father forgive your trespasses.* Matthew 6: 12, 14-15

Forgiveness is not a one-time thing; it is a daily forgiveness when I happen to think of something or a memory comes. Every time I have a new memory, I go through the process of being sad and feeling sorrow for my loss; I grieve that loss. I then forgive him for the pain created in me, and I can lay it at the foot of the cross and leave it there. It frees me from all the hostility. It no longer owns me as it has in the past and I rest in the freedom of what Jesus did for me and gave me.

Jesus gives us peace and leaves us His peace (John 14:27). I depend on those words so many times in my process of giving forgiveness. *If you know these things, blessed are you if you do them* (John 13:17). We are honored by God through Jesus for applying the Word of God.

Joyce Meyer says, "Doing the work is doing the Word." It is intentional work to live as an ongoing survivor. It is not a sometimes work. The enemy will look for any foothold to imprison us with anything he can use to suck us down into the pit; don't go there.

**I have a friend who says, "I will live responsibly, consciously and intentionally every day." That is my heart's desire and plan, too.**

All this seems simple in reading a chapter on forgiveness, but I assure you, it is not simple. And it is not easy. It is work, so be alert. It is through much prayer, time spent in relationship with Jesus, stillness, and vulnerability that these things are learned.

*Ask, and it will be given to you; seek, and you will find; knock and it will be opened to you.* Matthew 7:7

*The Forgiveness Factor, Finding Peace by Forgiving Others... and Yourself,* by Bruce Wilkerson, is an excellent book on seeking forgiveness. It identifies all the things that keep us in bondage. He helps the reader name those things and then complete the process of forgiveness.

We live in a complex world where things are glossed over or pushed under the rug, ignoring the things that should be faced. Anything that pains us, no matter how small, needs our attention or it will grow into a mountain. Molehills are much easier to forgive than years of pain and regret. It takes time; give yourself intentional time to forgive.

*In all your ways acknowledges Him and He will direct your path.*
Proverbs 3:6

*Let the words of my mouth and the meditation of my heart be acceptable in your sight, O LORD, my strength and my Redeemer.*
Psalm 19:14

**Don't give up and do not give in. Ask God's forgiveness for your sins so you may be set free.**

Eleven months before my dad passed away, I was in prayer and reading my Bible. I heard in my heart, "Call your dad, and ask him if he is going to heaven when he dies." I stated shaking and said, "Lord, how can I do such a thing?" He persisted. Two hours later after prayer and calling two friends to pray, I called. After a fear-filled conversation, he agreed to read the material I sent. Mom said he was different after that, but he never talked about it. No one ever knew the answer to my question to him; he didn't talk.

The movie *I Can Only Imagine*, gave me an excellent picture of a father who asked for forgiveness, even though my dad never acknowledged his sin against me or asked for forgiveness. I saw him in a new light. I saw him redeemed by Jesus, a free man from his sin. It was an amazing work of the Holy Spirit and I am more at peace now that I have ever been.

Don't get me wrong. This is very large process—a long, tedious, difficult, agonizing, and tearful process—in getting to this place of forgiveness. It is slow, one day at a time. Jesus is the one who walks with us on the journey. Only He can give us the courage and tenacity to walk this road.

*Father, I have tried so hard to work around forgiveness. I acknowledge my way does not work, but You have revealed to me Your perfect plan for forgiveness. I pray You help me to see my heart of sin through Your heart of love and all You have done for me. I trust You will show me from Your Word how to forgive all my sin because of the trauma and abuse, and how to believe You have cleansed me from all sin. Help me come to the place to forgive my abuser. I come to You, Lord Jesus. Amen.*

**Forgiveness – Matthew West**
https://www.youtube.com/watch?v=hiLu5udXEZI

# DAY 32: THE DIFFERENCE BETWEEN BEING A VICTIM AND A SURVIVOR

*For if you forgive men their trespasses, your heavenly Father will also forgive you. But if you do not forgive men their trespasses, neither will your Father forgive your trespasses.* Matthew 6:14-15

As a victim, we are subservient, we have no voice, we are invisible, and we do as we are told. As a survivor, we find our voice, we are now able to speak for ourselves, we take an active role, and we participate in life. With the changes from victim to survivor, we become a different person. We have learned who we are *not*, and *become* who God created us to be. Every person will be in a different place because everyone's story is different. It is between you and God to do the work.

In the beginning, I did it by sitting and just being, and God revealed himself to me through those quiet times. You may be different, and it is okay. But there is also another spectrum to deal with—your spouse.

After living many years as a victim this change is disruptive and uncertain to a spouse. It can be threatening to them. They do not know who we are, or what has happened to their world. They don't know this new person. Thus things become harder for the survivor, as well as difficult for the spouse. The survivor is now balancing a new life in thought and action, and not receiving support for the person they are becoming. Both husband and wife struggle to have a relationship with each other. This relational change happens when one person heals from traumatic experiences and is in the healing process, while the other person knows nothing of their world.

How do we as a survivor respond to the defensive role our spouse is now taking?

_____
_____
_____
_____
_____
_____
_____
_____

It takes much kindness and grace, which is hard to learn coming from a dysfunctional background and not seeing these qualities demonstrated. Our part as a survivor is dependence on Jesus to love with His love, speak with His grace, and respond with His kindness. It may be very difficult because it may not be received well. If we are not being abused physically or denied necessities, we must be filled with the Spirit of God to accomplish the task before us.

I can hear your first response—that is not fair! Who said

life would be fair? Jesus said, *"In this life we will have tribulation, but to be of good cheer, I have overcome the world. "* John 16:33

I too have been in this situation with a spouse who did not know who I now was and didn't know how to be in relationship with me. I had to come to some new terms as well, letting go of his defensive actions toward me. I had to forgive what was not known to him and, in turn, respond with kindness. My needs were not met. I was resentful, and I became angry and unforgiving. God had to get my attention to see what I had become because of all I had endured. It was not a pretty picture. The anger had turned to hatred and revenge from more than one person. There was so much to overcome.

When I saw my ugly self, I had much to repent for. It took time for my mind to change from a very bad attitude to one of thinking right and talking to myself about how I acted. It took time, prayer, and repentance asking God to change my attitude and heart to love with kindness and grace.

In turn, my husband had to learn where I was coming from, and he was angry for what had happened to me. We both had to let go, redevelop a communicative relationship, and express how we felt. This is the hard work of endurance and intentional actions, in order to develop new patterns for living with abuse issues. The anger, hatred, revenge, the scowling face, the bitterness, bad manners and bad behavior —all of it has to change to receive the attributes God has given each of us to offer to each other.

Time, prayer, trusting Jesus, knowing who God was, and knowing who I was in Christ were all a part of the healing process. It wasn't easy; it was intentional. I put on the armor of God to withstand the onslaught of the enemy. I put on the shield God offers to ward off the fiery darts of the enemy, and I used the sword of the Word to speak against the lies of the enemy, to be able to speak kindness and grace. I sought God's face to reflect Him instead of myself. It has changed my relationship with my husband, and our marriage went from turmoil to a place of peace.

God has done a mighty work in forgiving us, and we must extend the same grace to those who sin against us. This is powerful.

Can you extend forgiveness to someone who has hurt you deeply?

We must.

I want to be set free from this agony. I do not want to block my relationship with God. We can speak the words of forgiveness until our heart lines up with God's will, expressing the sorrow of an unforgiving spirit. I listed all the sins done against me and asked forgiveness one by one, coming to the place of forgiveness many times.

It takes time, prayerful seeking, confessing, and a willing heart to be set free. God's love soothed my soul and forgave me; the peace of God flooded my heart. I feel His peace. When an unsettled spirit creeps into my soul, I do not want to carry that load of unforgiveness. It is too heavy to carry.

We are always in the process of overcoming. It is ongoing, moment by moment trusting God for who we are in Christ. Without the truth of what Jesus did for us on the cross, we cannot be set free from what we believe as a result of our abuse. **We cannot do it on our own. God is the provider. Jesus is the only one who sets us free. Without Him, not one thing can be achieved.**

Are your heart, mind, and soul ready to hand over your unforgiving spirit?

Acknowledging you are a survivor instead of a victim is a vital part of your continued growth and victory over slavery. Giving up on any level of our healing and truth puts us back into victim mode. This is where we are used to living, we now no longer live there. You have come this far; do not give up or go back. Living in bondage is not trusting or believing the truth.

*Father, in the name of Jesus Christ, I depend on you to live as a survivor and thrive. Your redemption gives true freedom. Your grace and mercy are my greatest gift. I forgive those who have hurt me. I want to see those around me with "Jesus glasses," and to see that they need you just as I needed you. With a grateful heart, I keep my eyes on you. Thank you, Jesus, for new life. Amen.*

### Broken Girl – Matthew West
https://www.youtube.com/watch?v=VOYyi_FL79w

# DAY 33: WE ARE OVERCOMERS

*Blessed be the God and Father of Our Lord Jesus Christ, the Father of mercies and the God of all comfort, who comforts us in all our tribulation that we may be able to comfort those who are in any trouble, with the comfort with which we ourselves are comforted by God.* 2 Corinthians 1:3-4

I have been in ministry to sexually abused women for over seven years. I have talked to many women and men, who have shared their stories of harm, abuse, abandonment, neglect, and trauma. I have seen the love in a father's eyes for his daughter who was raped. I have heard the heartache of grandparents whose grandchildren were abused. Parents whose children are sexually assaulted ache in their hearts, wondering how their loved one will heal and how they can help.

The symptoms of abuse last a lifetime. The question is: How are we going to treat the symptoms and bring healing? Many times, the symptoms are not dealt with. Sometimes the symptoms are known, but how to deal with them is not. Sometimes adults do not remember their abuse because of the age at which the abuse started. Sometimes we do not know what the symptoms are. We pull ourselves up by the bootstraps, hang on by our fingernails, or tough it out. We live in denial or cover it with drugs, alcohol, sexual promiscuousness, adultery, cutting, eating disorders, busyness, or any number of things. These responses do not free us, and they do not fix the problem. They only gloss over the need to heal or add to the trauma already received. Healing comes with facing the issue head on.

The people who are set free have told someone, faced the truth, written their stories, trusted the Scriptures, found community with other survivors, forgiven the abusers, and currently live their lives on faith in a loving God. Many times, forgiveness comes in the latter part of healing. The people who do not face reality go back to where they were. Sometimes, even the ones who acknowledge their situation and know what Jesus did for them cannot accept the offer of grace. Tragically, their feelings of unworthiness or their deep anger is greater, which does not allow for healing or forgiveness.

**We cannot forgive until we know what we are forgiving.** It comes with forgiving one thing at a time. Quick forgiveness, hurriedly saying, "I forgive you," is not forgiveness. This glosses over the real depth of the issue and denies it, not seeking resolution. **We cannot resolve our issues not knowing what we are forgiving. The harm, the pain, and the abuse needs to be spoken.** We must say, "I forgive you for …" Forgiveness comes slowly to many people. As a new trigger comes to the surface, the process of forgiveness begins again. Forgive the new revelation of sin; lay it down at the foot of the cross. It must be grieved to heal from the loss. Sometimes forgiveness comes in layers. Do not be overwhelmed; trust God to reveal each step of forgiveness.

It is heartbreaking to see someone quit or not come to know Jesus Christ. Jesus is the one who paid for all sins, in order to release us from the burden and stain of it all. Our sin is covered by His blood, period. Nothing changes what He has already done for us. What does change is our response to it—our accepting God's gift of love and grace in Christ Jesus.

We have a choice. Choosing is hard for us because the enemy, Satan, makes us feel guilty and fearful and weak. God is using my story and your story to redeem you and others. Everyone has a story. We cannot redeem ourselves. We may think we can, but we cannot.

Loving God means loving my story. Do I love what happened to me? No, I do not love what happened to me, but because of what happened to me, I know God in a way I would never have known Him. I know without a shadow of a doubt that what happened to me was not my fault. It took me a very long time to accept and believe the facts. In seeking to find an answer, I was drawn to God. I love God, for caring for me and my story. My story brought me to the only one who could help me and cleanse me—Jesus Christ. God provided redemption through Jesus' death on the cross—that is what I love.

*From the end of the earth I will cry to You, when my heart is overwhelmed; lead me to the rock that is higher than I. For you have been a shelter to me, a strong tower from the enemy. I will abide in the Your tabernacle forever, I will trust in the shelter of Your wings.* Psalm 61:2-4

**God draws us to Himself to know Him; He is the Mighty God who loves us lavishly and kindly. He has a gift to offer us—He is offering His story of redemption in exchange for our story of pain.**

Will you trust God with your story?

What will you do to begin the process to know your own story well?

_____
_____
_____
_____
_____
_____
_____
_____

You may think I am not going deep enough. I am not. This is the tip of the iceberg. I am providing you with enough information to let you know it can be done, to encourage you to face the truth. It takes a lot of work, and you need faith to walk out and share your story. You need people in your life to walk this road with you, people to share your story with in community of believers. They need to hear your story.

Your faith and courage will grow as other are encouraged by your story of redemption. God always equips the ones He calls.

*Lord Jesus, you have brought me this far. I know you will lead me where you want me to share my story. I am an overcomer. I know you will walk with me when I am afraid. Hide me under your wing. Put the right people in my path and let me never give up. No matter what, I will keep my trust in you. In your name, amen.*

**Mandisa – Overcomer**
https://www.youtube.com/watch?v=b8VoUYtxokw

# DAY 34: GROWING IN GRACE

*May God bless you with His special favor and wonderful peace as you come to know Jesus, our God and Lord, better and better.* 2 Peter 1:2 NLT

This book will not go deep on any one subject. It is here to encourage you to keep on keeping on. I look back over all the years God has given me, and I am so thankful for God's faithfulness regardless of the messy days of emotional pain when I did not understand what I was going through. It is not easy to live as a survivor and thrive, but it is worth it.

God always provides in many different forms: It is a friend at the right time, not to answer a problem, but to listen and be there. It is a prayer, sermon, book, a moment or event. God surprises His beloved. He always provides what is needed when we need it. We are prompted by the Holy Spirit, resting in His spirit, trusting, knowing we are in His presence.

I enjoy the Daily Walk Bible, which has many translations for reading through the Bible in a year. It is amazing how it fits into a day by encouraging and teaching me how to apply the

Word, or by sustaining me in present issues. This helps me become familiar with God's character, His compassion for His people, His faithfulness, and His expectations.

Books are my treasures, the authors are my teachers, and I am in their classroom, broadening my horizons as they encourage and educate me. I never want to stop learning. *My Utmost for His Highest* is a great teaching book on daily living many times. The February ninth reading *Are You Physically Exhausted?* is for getting your strength from God. The February seventeenth day is for when you do not know what the next moment brings and the list goes on. There are many devotional books available to go along with daily Bible reading. Bible studies are another foundation for establishing faith.

Personal Bible study has gone hand in hand with group studies; without them, I would not have been grounded enough to do what I have done or am now doing. The relationships I have had with group members is so important. I love these women, who have been a great support throughout my life. I don't always see them, but often they have intersected with my journey unexpectedly. What a blessing they are to me.

**Life is not about just today; it is all the yesterdays and all the tomorrows. We do not want to burn bridges, but rather build relationship with God and with our fellow man. What a rich heritage we have! We need each other.**

Sometimes God uses the most interesting people in our lives, people who reach into our soul and change us for His good and our glory. They challenge us to think outside the box and to do that which keeps us growing. It keeps us on the path of being faithful to our calling. God has created each one of us in unique ways for unique purposes that only we can fill.

You may think of additional areas you would like to have

addressed. It would be good for you to write those pages for yourself. What an opportunity for you to go beyond where you are and to discover who God created you to be!

It has been my prayer to help wounded people on their journey. Our pain is never wasted when we are there for those who need encouragement.

It is never easy to share any story of abuse, but God gives the strength and courage to do so. I, myself, have been encouraged and comforted by many who have shared their story with me. I want to pass my story forward to all those who have been wounded, so that they too may be set free.

Redemption and freedom are gifts. I rejoice in the freedom from the prison I was in. There is nothing like freedom. My prayer is for everyone who reads this book to experience redemption and freedom. It is available to you no matter where you have been or who you have become or how old you are. It can all change if you desire it. It is your free gift, too.

*Jesus, I am so grateful for your grace in growing. You are here with me every minute through your Holy Spirit. You are transforming and growing my heart to be like yours. You provide what I need when I ask, lead me day by day with your Word, and pick me up when I fall, giving me confidence in you. Put actions to my heart's desire when I am not capable. I depend on you. Thank you for your redemption. I love you; you are beautiful, Lord. Amen.*

**Nobody Loves Me Like You – Chris Tomlin**
https://www.youtube.com/watch?v=SG_IXFEO8yE

## DAY 35: WHOSE STORY HAVE YOU HEARD?

*As you therefore have received Christ Jesus, the Lord, so walk in Him, rooted and built up in Him and established in the faith, as you have been taught, abounding in it with thanksgiving.*
Colossians 2:6-7

In my infancy as a believer, I was in a women's Sunday school class led by Mrs. Griffin. I loved this class. She showed her heart and taught me to hang onto God's Word daily. I can still see her in my mind at the front of the class reciting Scripture of what God had done for her. She shared Psalm 40:2-3.

*He has brought me up out of the horrible pit, out of the miry clay, and set my feet upon a rock, and established my steps. He has put a new song in my mouth- praise to our God; many will see it and fear, and will trust in the Lord.*

She said, "If God can do that for me, He can do that for you." She didn't know at the time how much I needed to hear those words.

I memorized the verses written on small pieces of paper she passed out each week, reciting them over and over in my hurting world. I was inspired so many times through the years from the echo her faith displayed in those days.

*So shall My word be that goes forth from My mouth; it shall not **return** to Me **void**, but it shall accomplish what I please, and it shall prosper in the thing for which I sent it.* Isaiah 55:11

One of the verses I received from her was 1 Corinthians 15:58: *Therefore, my beloved brethren, be steadfast, immovable, always abounding in the work of the Lord, knowing that your labor is not in vain in the Lord.* Be steadfast! For me that was a powerful statement. At the time, I was in crisis emotionally, and it gave me courage to face the pain I was in. It meant never give up, never stop trying, never stop believing that God would take care of me, no matter where I was or what I was doing.

**Believing God has proved to be the faithful thing to do. God is faithful when we believe all that He says in His Word.**

*The Lord is my strength and my shield; my heart trusts in Him, and I am helped; therefore my heart greatly rejoices and with my song I will praise Him.* Psalm 28:7

**My song is— "Thank you, Lord, for the women who have gone before me, who share their faith in You and who tell of Your great goodness to them so that I might believe Your promises are mine too."**

Whose story have you heard, telling you of God's great goodness to them that you might believe?

What verse from God's Word has given you hope and encouragement?

_____
_____
_____
_____
_____
_____
_____
_____

Write it down and memorize it. It will be your encouragement to never give up, never stop trying, and never stop believing that God loves you and will take care of you. The testimony of another believer is powerful in our life as we see God working in their life, and it gives us hope that He is doing the same for us.

Looking back through the years, I see how God worked behind the scenes in my life. He is doing the same for you.

We think God doesn't care, but He is working to bring you to Himself. He created you in His image, and He has a plan for you, to prosper you and give you hope.

*For I know the plans I have for you, declares the Lord, plans to prosper you and not to harm you, plans to give you a hope and a future.* Jeremiah 29:11 NIV

*Father, give me a verse I can hang onto and never give up. Amen.*

**With My Lips I Will Praise You – Twila Paris**
https://www.youtube.com/watch?v=l38DRxfJ5fQ

# DAY 36: HOW TO RESPOND TO ANOTHER PERSON'S STORY

*But she answered him, "No my brother, do not force me, for no such things should be done in Israel. Do not do this disgraceful thing! And I, where could I take my shame?"* 2 Samuel 13:12-13

This is the story about Ammon, who sexually assaulted his half-sister, Tamar. It is a sad story. In that day, Ammon could have married Tamar, but Ammon wanted instant gratification for his sexual imaginations. He would not listen to Tamar and her father, King David, did nothing to protect or defend her after the attack.

Yes, good questions to ask are, "Where do I take my shame when I have been forced by a sexual assault or sexually abused? Who will listen to me, much less believe me? Who can I trust?"

We as abused and assaulted people are in the same place as Tamar. When we share our story of abuse or trauma, will we be heard and validated? Sometimes the hearer of our story has been triggered because of their own story.

The storyteller is trusting that the Holy Spirit has led them to share their story with you. They are being vulnerable and open with their heart in telling another person. They are trusting it is heard by a reliable person who will respond well. However, do not take it personally if they do not; it is not about you if they do not respond.

I have seen blank stares, or the subject has been changed because the hearer does not know how to respond.

The proper response is validating the person who shared. "Thank you for sharing your story," or, "You are a very courageous person to have come through..."

Listen for the shame messages; when you hear a shame message, use kind words. Be aware of your body language. Offer kind eyes and face; don't be shocked. Don't hold back your tears, because connecting to their heart is comforting. Tears are necessary for healing. Speak from your heart to their pain by telling them you believe them. Affirm their inherent dignity as an image bearer of God. Look for evidence of glory. Where is the storyteller strong, bold, tender, kind, or delightfully alive? Validate or affirm the storyteller; they need to hear you respond. Silence is deafening to a storyteller, and shame is easy to feel from a silent hearer.

Learning how to respond to stories can feel intimidating. The following are examples of good responses:

- Thank you for sharing your story.
- You are a courageous person to share so honestly.
- Your abuse was not your fault.
- I am sad about what happened to you.
- What was done to you was bad; I don't see you as bad.
- I hate what was done to you.
- I don't think any less of you for what you have shared with us; thank you for trusting us.
- You had no one to protect you and I am so sorry.

You had a right to be angry about_____.
\*Adapted from the Journey, Open Heart Ministry. www.ohmin.org Used with permission.

**Your words of care and compassion are respectful to the storyteller. They have been shamed and belittled many times in their life. It takes courage to share their story. They may wonder if they were heard; your validation is a blessing and a kindness.** A proper response is a gift to them, as they have given you a gift of sharing their story with you. We never know who will be blessed by our being vulnerable in sharing our story. It gives hope and courage to so many others who did not know they could tell their story and may be one day set free as the storyteller has. That is the hope of the storyteller.

*It is for freedom that Christ has set us free.* Galatians 5:1

**Listen well when someone tells you their story.**

*Father give me ears to hear and eyes to see the person who is telling me their story. I pray to see the beauty of Christ and the image of God in them. Help me to validate them and give them dignity. It took boldness to trust me with their story. I am blessed that they cared to tell me what you have done in their life and that they encouraged me. In Jesus' Name, amen.*

**I Stand in Awe of You - Chris Tomlin**
https://www.youtube.com/watch?v=TZrvLRgHaVY

## DAY 37: WRITE YOUR STORY

*For everything that was written in the past was written to teach us, so that through endurance and the encouragement of the Scriptures we might have hope.* Romans 15:4 NIV

Writing your story may be a new thought for you, and it may seem hard and impossible. We have no idea it will make such a difference, but writing our story gives us a visual picture that helps the pieces fall into place. It gives us the ability to see more than we have ever seen before.

You are beginning a new journey in seeking healing and freedom in your heart and mind. A new beginning may seem scary, but look at it as a new day. Every day is a new day, a fresh start. **You may think you do not have a story to tell, but you do.**

Start with where you were born, where you lived as a child, who your siblings are, and where you went to school. Write what you remember. Do not worry about spelling or punctuation; just write. The words will spill out through your pen as you write. You will remember things you haven't thought about in years. Each little bit of information is key to your healing, key to unlocking the past. Everything is important.

Give yourself twenty minutes to write, and then stop. Later, continue from where you left off. This helps keep the task from overwhelming you. Ask God to help you write;. He knows all about you, and He will listen to your pleas and guide your thoughts.

*You comprehend my paths and my lying down, and are acquainted with all my ways.* Psalm 139:3

*...God is greater than our heart and knows all things.* 1 John 3:20

It is statistically proven that writing is healing for our brains. Our brain is deeply affected by harm; your brain will begin to heal as you write. Writing is a place of discovery. Dr. Caroline Leaf's book on *Who Switched Off My Brain?* is helpful in understanding how much abuse and trauma affects the brain. It also explains how the brain can heal itself by releasing the bad chemicals from bad thoughts, by starting to thinking good thoughts with the good chemicals flowing through our brain.

We find out who we are when we write our story. We begin to feel again, and we are able to use new words to describe how we feel. For most abuse victims, our feelings are deeply buried, and writing brings them back to the surface. Be aware of how you feel and how your mind is starting to think, and you will discover yourself. Bad thoughts are a poison in our bodies. Like an infection, it needs to come out of our minds and bodies.

Use the Feeling Word Chart at the end of this book to find the word or words you need to express yourself.

I watched a demonstration of making a story quilt on television. The woman used her grandmother as a key figure in her quilt. She wrote down twenty-two things she remembered about her grandmother. As she worked on the quilt over the weeks, she remembered more details and continued writing more memories, even the smallest details. She created a beautiful quilt in remembrance of a woman who influenced her life so much. It doesn't matter what project you are working on when you write your story; the more you process the more you will remember.

Don't think it is all negative; there is good to be found even if we think we do not have good memories. The memories you remember are key factors that give clarity in your story. Work on it for healing, and you will be set free in remembering the details. As our story is revealed, we gain back our personal power. We see who God created us to be, receive our lives back, and recover the things stolen from us. It is a process requiring time.

**We who have been silenced gain personal strength and power as we see the person God created us to be. The truth sets us free. Redemption becomes real.** Our dependency upon Christ releases us from trying to solve or fix our problems. God has the responsibility of caring for us, which He is doing.

*He reveals deep and secret things; He knows what is in the darkness, and light dwells with Him.* Daniel 2:22

*The Lord is my light and my salvation, whom shall I fear? The Lord is the strength of my life; of whom shall I be afraid.* Psalm 27:1

We come to the place where we no longer fear the

unknown of our lives. Knowing our story gives us words of truth, including words about the harm done to us;. It frees us and heals our wounded heart, soul, and mind. There is power in speaking the truth.

I started writing my story eleven years ago; it has been added to many times. As I have been healed and been set free, more details have been revealed—the ones too deep to cope with at first. God's Word and His Presence have always guided me. I now ask, "What do you want me to know?" Check the triggers—a sound, a word, something that provoked the memory. I ask, "What do I believed about the provoked memory? Is it true? If it is not true, what is the lie?" Identify the lie, seeking the truth from God. Don't hurry. Wait. It takes time to process. God, in His mercy, is gracious and kind, guiding and directing. He doesn't give you more than you can handle for the moment.

Our story happened one day and one event at a time. Because abuse is traumatic, we are confused about many things. Writing gives us order and helps us remember things we have forgotten or have not thought about for a long time. Also, read your journal. It is surprising the insight you have written down that you haven't connected with before.

**Everything you remember is important. Memories are critical. When the right circumstance arise, we are able to put together the pieces of our story.**

I thank God for the grace extended to me in this process of continued and ongoing healing. I am blessed, and I walk in freedom. I pray every reader will be set free from the pain of the abuse and trauma they have gone through. Freedom is the best place in the whole world to live.

Will you start today to write your story?

What is keeping you from writing your story?

Will you trust the One who made you and created you for beauty?

Find a Scripture, write it down, and memorize it. Repeat it often, so it fills you with courage.

_____
_____
_____
_____
_____
_____
_____
_____

*Lord Jesus, the thought of writing my story is scary, but I will. I depend on you to be my shield and refuge, to help me not be fearful. Knowing you created me for glory, that the image of Christ is in me, I know I am filled with your Holy Spirit. I trust you to guide me. You have done more than I ever dreamed. What a great God and Lord you are to care about and love me before I was born! I cannot comprehend such great love. Give me opportunity to tell your story with my story. Thank you, Jesus. You are beautiful. Amen.*

**My Story, Big Daddy Weave**
https://www.youtube.com/watch?v=1TKAN-nAsu8

# DAY 38: THERE WILL BE OPPOSITION

*Consider him who endured such opposition from sinners, so that you will not grow weary and lose heart.* Hebrews 12:3 NIV

It is especially true for survivors of sexual abuse that when we are set free we will have opposition. The enemy will use the smallest thing to make us doubt. An old fear comes back. Or we experience shame, ambivalence, self-contempt, hatred, anger—so many struggles. We retreat; we are afraid of the unknown and uncertainty. Anytime we live in truth, things will happen. It is especially true for sexual abuse survivors. Without thinking through what has just happened, we retreat. We are afraid of the unknown and uncertainty. Doubt takes hold, and we begin to think we are wrong, that it is our fault. We get confused and cannot think straight.

Shame belittles us. We play the "would've and could've" game. If we would just be better, be quiet, or have done something else, everything would be alright. I should have done more, or if I would have been on time, or 'whatever else... (you fill in the words)—then all would be good.

Wrong!

Opposition will bring all this to our minds.

Stop.

Look back. Remember what God has revealed. Speak the truth. The enemy wants to scramble your brain. **Lean on the promises the Lord has taught you.** Recite the verses you have learned. Stand firm in the grace and in the knowledge of the fight you have gone through.

Jesus said, *"In the world you will have tribulations, but be of good cheer, I have overcome the world."* (John 16:33) We cannot do this alone; we need spiritual strength to stand up for ourselves and speak.

*Finally, my brethren, be strong in the Lord and in the power of His might. Ephesians 6:10*

*We have previously suffered and been insulted in Philippi, as you know, but with the help of our God we dared to tell you his gospel in the face of strong opposition.* 1 Thessalonians 2:2 NIV

**We are not alone. God is with us.**

We are in a spiritual war with the enemy, but he has lost ground. Align yourself with the Word of God, stand on the truth of what God says, use your armor, and fight with the weapon of Scripture.

Because you have dared to share your story, receive redemption, and proclaim your salvation, you are the bullseye for attack. Keep your guard up; it is never safe to think you have arrived. The enemy is looking for the smallest crack in your armor to shoot his fiery darts and catch you off guard.

You are now thriving. There is nothing greater. You are in relationship with the living God, communing with Him moment by moment. You are free, laughing, and enjoying life.

See the good in people and in the things that used to upset you. Make choices, speak up, know who you are, and most of all, know who you are not.

What a great place to be.

You are now thriving.

**Living as a survivor is a daily choice with the guidance of the Holy Spirit, faithful friends, and prayer. We are warriors of the faith. We are in battle against the powers of darkness and we will stand. (Ephesians 6:10-18) Rejoice in this.**

*Blessed be the God and Father of our Lord Jesus Christ, who has blessed us with every spiritual blessing in the heavenly places in Christ.* Ephesians 1:3

*Father, opposition is hard; I cannot stand against it on my own. Go before me. I trust and believe who I am in you. Give me understanding as I read the Bible; show me what the Holy Spirit is revealing. Give me courage to speak. I have choices, and I believe who you say I am—worthy to be loved. I put my armor on, standing firm, and using my voice to share your great love, enjoying life being who you created me to be in Christ Jesus. I will proclaim my redemption. Jesus, I thank you. Amen.*

**Stand Up for Jesus with lyrics. An old hymn of the church with powerful words.**
https://www.youtube.com/watch?v=r11Gmdq__-8

## DAY 39: WHO KNOWS?

*Who knows...* Esther 4:14

The story of Esther has always stirred my heart with its contrast of Esther's journey from being a peasant girl to becoming the Queen of Persia. She was adopted by her Uncle Mordecai, as her parents had died (2:7). She was kidnapped along with many other beautiful young women by the king's officers in order to find a suitable woman to replace Queen Vashti, who had disobeyed the king's orders of parading before his drunken friends at a party.

Esther was then put under the custody of Hegai, the custodian of the women. She completed twelve months of preparation according to the regulations of the women who were to spend one night with the king. She would not go in to the king again unless he delighted in her.

As it was, Esther pleased him and obtained his favor. She did not reveal her people or family, for Mordecai had charged her not to reveal it. Haman, who was in the king's court sat above all the princes and everyone bowed to him except Mordecai, Esther's uncle. Mordecai did not bow or pay homage because he was a Jew. Haman wanted to eliminate all the Jews, and he set out to convince the king to proclaim an edict to set in motion their extermination. Letters were sent to every province, being published for all the people, instructing them to be ready for that day.

When Mordecai learned all that had happened, he sat in sackcloth by the king's gate. Esther was informed, and he asked Esther to petition the king for their lives.

> *And Mordecai answered to Esther: "Do not think in your heart that you will escape in the King's palace any more than all the other Jews. For if you remain completely silent at this time, relief and deliverance will arise for the Jews from another place, but you and your father's house will perish. Yet <u>who knows</u> whether you have come to the kingdom for such a time as this." Esther 4:13-14*

**"Who knows?" What a good question. "Who knows?" Maybe it is why you have read this book for your survival. The question is—do you want freedom more than complacency?**

When we are complacent, we do not stand up for ourselves. Any person who harms another is very good at manipulation and will silence you. We lose our voice, we cannot stand up for ourselves, nor do not know we can. The only hope in standing up for ourselves is to tell a safe person, seek help, and remove ourselves from the situation. We can do a lot for ourselves by getting angry about our harm and abuse. It is our right to get angry.

After three days of prayer and fasting, Esther went to the king without an invitation, in order to save the Jews and herself from annihilation. She said, "If I perish, I perish." When the king saw Queen Esther standing in the court, he held out the golden scepter that was in his hand and said to her, "What do you wish?"

Are you willing to hold out your hand to God Almighty, Jesus the King, and ask Him your request for freedom?

In God's providence, He will put the right people into your life. This is a walk of believing faith and trust in the only One who can truly set you free.

Esther was a woman of courage under great pressure. Through Mordecai, who is a picture of the Holy Spirit, Esther realized that her life had greater purpose than her own comfort. She trusted that God was able to save her. She believed that through prayer and fasting she could do what she knew was right, not only for herself, but also for all the people she represented.

One person represents many who are suffering from sexual abuse and trauma. Others did it for me; I am now doing it for you.

Four and a half years after I learned the truth, I had the courage to tell my story. I spoke the words of my abuse. God gave me the boldness I did not know I had. I committed my life to help other sexual abuse survivors. I was set free not only for myself, but also for all those who, like myself, have been harmed by sexual abuse and trauma. I did not know, nor did it matter, what that journey looked like. I committed myself and trusted God through the Holy Spirit's guidance one moment at a time.

All the years I spent in Bible study, reading books, and attending seminars, God was preparing me for what I am now doing—speaking, educating, doing classes, writing my blog and writing this book, encouraging and praying for people. Am I qualified? Not according to the standards of the world. God has reminded me over and over, "I taught you." I have no excuse. My answer is, 'Who knows, but that God has called me for such a time as this."

> *Now then, we are ambassadors for Christ, as though God were pleading through us; we implore you on Christ's behalf, be reconciled to God.* 2 Corinthians 5:20

> *My sheep hear My voice, and I know them, and they follow me.* John 10:27

> *But what things were gain to me, these I have counted loss for Christ. Yet indeed I also count all things loss for the excellence of the knowledge of Christ Jesus my Lord, for whom I have suffered the loss of all things and count them rubbish, that I may gain Christ.* Philippians 3:7-8

Believe God loves you. Without believing God loves you, you will not love yourself. You are worth loving. Let God love you, and receive all He has to offer you. Let Him reveal who He created you to be and reveal the image of Christ in you. You are filled with the glory of God. Let it shine through you.

Will you have the courage to share your story?

_____
_____
_____
_____
_____
_____
_____
_____

*Who knows* – you could!

*Heavenly Father, you know my story, you know my heart, and you know my pain. Help me, and give me courage. I want to stand up and share my story. Who knows, maybe this is the time for me to stand up for myself and say "no" to abuse, "no" to all this pain, "no" to anything that is holding me back from sharing my story. Who knows what I can do that I never thought I could. Esther was a woman of faith. Let me follow in her footsteps, speaking the truth about sexual abuse, and the harm it causes to follow you, even as I live in a life of freedom. Thank You, Jesus. Amen.*

## Lead Me, Lord – Gary Valenianco
https://www.youtube.com/watch?v=76KsgvKrqnI

# DAY 40: SAY "YES" TO GOD

*Come and hear, all you who fear God, and I will declare what He has done for my soul.* Psalm 66:16

Recently a friend told me a story about herself. She was rehearsing her story with another friend in preparation for sharing with a larger group of people. After she shared her story, she said, "I do not know why out of all my family I am the only one who God has given His grace to and set me free from all this pain in my life." Her friend said, "You said 'yes' to God."

**You said "yes" to God! What a powerful statement.**

We must say **"yes"**, or we will not be set free. What was meant for evil will now be changed to what is meant for good. You said **"yes"** to redemption. What a glorious day! Jesus has been calling you, and you can finally respond and say **"yes"** That is a very big deal!

**The big deal is God exchanged our pain for his healing.** Romans 6 is the best chapter for telling us we are dead to sin and alive to God. This is because Jesus died for us and the power of His resurrection set us free from the power of sin and death. Verse 4 – *Therefore we are buried with Him through baptism into death, that just as Christ was raised from the dead by the glory of the Father, even so we also should walk in newness of life.*

There are three powerful key words in Romans 6, know, count (or reckon), and yield (depending which version of the Bible you are using.). Verse 6 of the NIV says, *"and we <u>know</u> that our old self was crucified with him so that the body of sin might be rendered powerless, that we should no longer be slaves to sin."*

Verse 11 of the NIV says *"in the same way, **count (reckon)** yourselves dead to sin but alive to God in Christ Jesus."*

Verse 13 of the NIV says *"do not **offer (yield or present)** the parts of your body to sin, as instruments of wickedness, but rather offer yourselves to God, as those who have been brought from death to life: and offer the parts of your body to him as instruments of righteousness."*

These three words are easily remembered: **know** that Jesus died for you; you can say **no** to sin. You can **count** on him. You can **yield** to God instead of to sin and unrighteousness.

This truth has carried me though many times of uncertainly and doubt, and has saved me from much trouble.

Spend time studying this chapter. Know what God has provided for you and what you can depend on. *I will never leave you nor forsake you. (Hebrews 13:5)* The power of the Word gives us what is needed, in contrast with the old way, which only sucks us deeper into old patterns of thinking and doing instead of overcoming.

> *So then, just as you have received Christ Jesus, continue to live in Him, rooted and built up in him, strengthened in faith as you were taught, overflowing with thankfulness.* Colossians 2:6-7 NIV

Saying **"yes"** to God has changed my life. And it has not only changed mine, but also the lives of many with whom I have the privilege of sharing my story. All of us are in a new place, experiencing new hope, having new anticipation, and seeing new results.

Saying **"yes"** to God is a moment by moment decision involving overcoming, choosing, depending on the Word of God, and believing the truths God has provided through the power of the Holy Spirit. This is breaking the old sin nature and relishing the blessings of trusting in Jesus to free us.

Will you say **"yes"** to God?

Will you say the words out loud to God?

_____

_____

_____

_____

_____

_____

_____

_____

I pray you will act today and allow God to set you free from the bondage of any kind of abuse and trauma. Share you story. Give God glory. This is the most wonderful, beautiful gift you could ever receive, well worth the effort and work. It infuses you with the power of the Holy Spirit! Speaking words of life to all who will hear.

It takes time, grace, and giving yourself kindness and space, because healing is ongoing throughout your whole life.

Have key verses, repeating them as you need them. Add new verses as changes occur; they will be your courage and strength to move forward in all God has created you for.

*Lord Jesus, I count myself alive to you. I yield myself and my story to you as you continue to heal me from my trauma and pain, giving me strength and courage through your Word. I say, "yes" to you with my life and my voice. Use me to tell my story of your redemption to whomever, wherever, and whenever, for your glory. I pray in your wonderful, powerful name. Amen.*

**I Am Set Free – All Sons and Daughters**
https://www.youtube.com/watch?v=I3_Py-6eRqI

# AFTERWORD

*How blessed is God! And what a blessing he is! He's the Father of our Master, Jesus Christ, and takes us to the high places of blessing in him. Long before he laid down earth's foundations, he had us in mind, had settled on us as the focus of his love, to be made whole and holy by his love. Long, long ago he decided to adopt us into his family through Jesus Christ. (What pleasure he took in planning this!) He wanted us to enter into the celebration of his lavish gift-giving by the hand of his beloved Son.* Ephesians 1:3-6 MSG

Living as a survivor and thriving on a daily basis is the purpose of this book. I have given you a taste of freedom. It is possible. Our heart's desire motivates us to be in relationship with Jesus every day. It drives us to our knees in thanksgiving, spending time with the One who redeemed us. It gives us hearts filled with joy that we did not experience before. He lavishes us with His love and character. Does this mean we will never have a bad day or miss a time of fellowship with Jesus? No, we are not perfect. Life is too volatile to expect perfection. This isn't about perfection; it is about relationship.

We need Jesus every day, and we need to be in community with one another.

My prayer through this book is for God to reveal through His Holy Spirit a desire for freedom, as well as a desire to practice His truths and principles and develop your own personal relationship with Jesus Christ. Everyone is made in the image of God. He has a plan specifically designed for you like no other. He wants you to say "yes," and follow His leading. God opens doors and closes doors for our good and for His purpose.

I knew God called me to minister, but I did not know it would be to those who are sexually abused. He has equipped and led me through one thing at a time.

It started by sharing my story. Through a Bible study, a door opened to start a ministry called Beloved Ministry. In this ministry, I led classes to show how to overcome once people know about the abuse. I wrote my own material and was then introduced to Dr. Dan Allender's book *The Wounded Heart*. After two sessions using Dan's workbook on *The Wounded Heart*, I met Gina Gronberg, doing *The Journey* workbook from Open Heart Ministry.

Trained at Maranatha by Open Heart Ministry and mentored by Gina Gronberg, I have lead Journey classes since that time. A young woman, Gracie Kelley, set up a blog for me. A blog? I did not know what a blog was. We laugh about it now, because I started writing a blog.

Janet Smith then edited for me and her husband, Dan, managed the blog, which led me to the Colorado Christian Writer's Conference in Estes Park.

God has brought many people along the pathway of thriving who have encouraged and prayed and given financially to this book. It couldn't have happened without God leading the way. I thank and praise My God and Savior Jesus Christ.

I count it a privilege and honor to represent the One who sets me free, sharing God's story in telling my story. Coming out of the fog into the daylight about my own personal journey has been the journey of my life. It is hard and raw, but it changed everything. Hiding away is not an option; I knew I did not survive just for me. I want to help as many people as possible who are in the same darkness of sexual abuse I was in. It is not a place to live; it is pure hell.

If I can come out of the darkness and lies, I promise, you can too. You may think you can't, but you can. If you want freedom, the freedom Jesus has to offer you, you can do it. It may be hard and long, but it is worth every day of freedom. If there is anything I have said that has helped, I am happy; it is a place of new beginnings.

My prayer is for you to be courageous and bold, and to accept the offer God made available through Jesus Christ—the road less traveled, the journey to freedom. You are not alone. You are who God created you to be—beautiful and filled with His glory, with a special purpose. You make a difference.

*The Lord bless you and keep you; the Lord make His face shine upon you and be gracious to you; the Lord lift up is countenance upon you and give you His peace. Amen* Numbers 6:4-6

Yes, you can. Yes, you can.

*Father, thank you for the privilege of sharing your story of love through my story. I pray every person who reads it is encouraged, taking a new step of faith each day. Give them renewed hope, and a life full of joy and freedom. You said you are the light of the world; may they walk in your light through every moment of the day. Help them see the invisible God, Jesus their advocate, declaring them not guilty, forgiven, and free. Together we praise you in your Name, for you are our Redeemer, faithful and true. In Jesus' precious name, be glory forever and ever. Amen.*

## On Eagle's Wings

https://www.youtube.com/watch?v=MvpjxfWrjzY

# ABOUT THE AUTHOR

Janet Feil speaks to groups and is involved with *Find Our Voice Symposiums* to educate and inform the public about sexual abuse. She has a passion to help people live in freedom from all of the lies they believe about themselves because of sexual abuse.

Visit her online at https://belovedministries.net

# ACKNOWLEDGMENTS

In authoring this book, I, the writer was only one of many to accomplish this task. It takes many talented people to develop, edit, format, create and do many other things I do know how to do.

I will begin with Grace Kelley, who was on my developing team for Beloved Ministries in the summer of 2010. Being a young college student, she knew computer technology and developed a blog for me when I didn't know what a blog was. It was the beginning of my writing career. She also edited for me until she graduated from Colorado State University.

Janet Smith became my editor and taught me many things about writing. Her husband Dan Smith maintained the blog site, without which I could not have done without.

Gina Gronberg mentored me in The Journey Begins, a workbook taking me through the life-changing work to freedom from survivor to thriving.

Michelle Ramus, my co-leader and prayer partner for the last seven years, who without, I would not have gotten this far on my journey, meet weekly for prayer and encouragement and waiting on God for his plan for us, has been a blessed adventure in faith and trust.

Colorado Christian Writer's Conference, in Estes Park, Colorado, under the leadership of Marlene Bagnull, put me into a new world of being an author, of which I have attended since 2014, meeting people from the literary world that have enlarged my borders and territory to new heights.

Penelope Kay - Penny Hudson, a fellow writer, author of *Making Crooked Places Straight,* who I met at the Writer's Conference helped me with all the in's and out's of writing, computer technology, and the next step.

I want to thank my editor, Debbie Maxwell Allen, Good Catch Publishing, for all her patience in editing my book and answering my many questions and for all the setup work on Amazon and Ingram Spark. Bethany Grove, The Word Jeanie for proofreading, Gale Schadewald – GaleForce Design, for the book cover design. Tamara O'dell — Tamara O'Dell PR and Marketing, for writing the back cover. Sharon Hartman – Photography by Hartman for my picture, and M Sanders for updating the Beloved Ministries website. To the many friends too numerous to mention for fear I would miss someone from this wonderful group of people, you know who you are, thank you for lifting me up in prayer and encouraged me through the process of writing. Special thanks to Linda and Mike Prenzlow, Bob and Jeane Foster, Mike and Dorothy Vaughan, my brother and his wife -Greg and Sue Hoffman, for support and prayers as well.

I thank my husband, Gary, for his patience in the many hours I spent on my computer and my family's encouragement.

I praise and thank God, Jesus Christ, my Savior, and the Holy Spirit's presence as I wrote, giving me scripture and the topic to write on, as I waited on him to direct me.

Janet Feil

# RECOMMENDED BOOK LIST

*The Wounded Heart*, Dr. Dan Allender
*Healing the Wounded Heart*, Dr. Dan Allender
*Bold Love*, Dr. Dan Allender and Dr. Tremper Longman III
*To Be Told*, Dr. Dan Allender
*Who Switched Off My Brain?: Controlling Toxic Thoughts and Emotions*, Dr. Caroline Leaf
*Switch On Your Brain, The Key to Peak Happiness, Thinking, and Health*, Dr. Caroline Leaf
*Victory Over the Darkness: Realize the Power of Your Identity in Christ*, Dr. Neil Anderson
*Winning Your Daily Spiritual Battles*, Linda Evans Shepherd
*The Freedom Factor: Finding Peace by Forgiving others... and Yourself*, Dr. Bruce Wilkinson
*When A Woman You Love Was Abused*, Dawn Scott Jones
Strong's Concordance

**Devotionals**

*God's Best Secrets* – Andrew Murray
*My Utmost for His Highest* – Oswald Chambers
*Streams in the Dessert* – Mrs. Charles Cowan

## JOURNEY GROUPS

*The Journey Begins* was written by Open Heart Ministry, Kalamazoo, Michigan. www.ohmin.org. The website will give information where classes are being held within the United States. Attend a class in your area. Leadership training is available plus much more.

'The Journey Begins is a nine-week workbook taking you through the past - the road you have been on, the present - the road you are on, and the future – the road ahead.

> *'to a healing journey...*
> *an experience where you can explore your story and*
> *find your heart...*
> *to a community of fellow travelers...*
> *people seeking to be real, to dream, to come alive...*
> *to an environment of grace, truth, and affirmation...*
> *a safe place to look at the past and discover a*
> *future...*
> *to a fresh relationship with the Wounded Healer...*
> *a God who knows, cares and is intimately*
> *involved...*

*come along with us on a journey of transformation."\**

\*Used by permission from Open Heart Ministry

## BOOKS MENTIONED

*When Trust is Lost* by Dr. Dan Allender (page 4)

*Victory over the Darkness* by Neil Anderson (page 66)

*How People Change* by Paul Tripp (page 69)

*The Wounded Heart* by Dr. Dan Allender (page 78)

*Streams in the Desert* by Mrs. Charles E. Cowman (page 96)

*Who Switched Off My Brain? Controlling Toxic Thoughts and Emotions* by Dr. Caroline Leaf (page 97)

*Who Switched On My Brain? The Key to Peak Happiness, Thinking, and Health* by Dr. Caroline Leaf (page 97)

*The Rest of God* by Mark Buchanan (page 104)

*The Forgiveness Factor, Finding Peace by Forgiving Others...and Yourself* by Bruce Wilkerson (page 109)

The Daily Walk Bible (page 118)
    *My Utmost for His Highest* by Oswald Chambers (page 118)

*The Journey* by Open Heart Ministry (page 139)

# FEELING WORDS CHART: POSITIVE

*Love*
*Open*
*Happy*
*Alive*
*Good*
*Interested*
*Positive*
*Strong*
*Loving*
*Understanding*
*Joyous*
*Playful*
*Calm*
*Concerned*
*Eager*
*Sure*
*Considerate*
*Confident*
*Fortunate*

## Feeling Words Chart: Positive

*Courageous*
*Peaceful*
*Affected*
*Intent*
*Certain*
*Affectionate*
*Reliable*
*Delighted*
*Energetic*
*At Ease*
*Fascinated*
*Anxious*
*Unique*
*Sensitive*
*Easy*
*Overjoyed*
*Liberated*
*Comfortable*
*Intrigued*
*Inspired*
*Dynamic*
*Tender*
*Amazed*
*Gleeful*
*Optimistic*
*Pleased*
*Encouraged*
*Absorbed*
*Determined*
*Tenacious*
*Devoted*
*Free*
*Thankful*

## Feeling Words Chart: Positive

*Provocative*
*Clever*
*Inquisitive*
*Excited*
*Hardy*
*Attracted*
*Sympathetic*
*Important*
*Impulsive*
*Surprised*
*Nosy*
*Enthusiastic*
*Secure*
*Passionate*
*Interested*
*Festive*
*Giddy*
*Content*
*Snoopy*
*Bold*
*Empowered*
*Admiration*
*Satisfied*
*Ecstatic*
*Animated*
*Quiet*
*Engrossed*
*Brave*
*Ambitious*
*Warm*
*Receptive*
*Satisfied*
*Spirited*

*Relaxed*
*Intense*
*Daring*
*Powerful*
*Touched*
*Accepting*
*Glad*
*Thrilled*
*Serene*
*Curious*
*Challenged*
*Confident*
*Sympathy*
*Kind*
*Cheerful*
*Wonderful*
*Free & Easy*
*Friendly*
*Optimistic*
*Bold*
*Close*
*Amiable*
*Sunny*
*Generous*
*Bright*
*Caring*
*Re-enforced*
*Determined*
*Loved*
*Appreciated*
*Elated*
*Goofy*
*Blessed*

*Confident*
*Comforted*
*Jubilant*
*Reassured*
*Hopeful*

# FEELING WORDS CHART: NEGATIVE

*Angry*
*Depressed*
*Confused*
*Helpless*
*Indifferent*
*Afraid*
*Hurt*
*Sad*
*Irritated*
*Lousy*
*Upset*
*Incapable*
*Insensitive*
*Fearful*
*Crushed*
*Tearful*
*Enraged*
*Disappointed*
*Doubtful*
*Alone*

*Dull*
*Terrified*
*Tormented*
*Sorrowful*
*Hostile*
*Discouraged*
*Uncertain*
*Paralyzed*
*Nonchalant*
*Suspicious*
*Deprived*
*Pained*
*Sore*
*Ashamed*
*Indecisive*
*Fatigued*
*Neutral*
*Alarmed*
*Tortured*
*Grieved*
*Annoyed*
*Powerless*
*Perplexed*
*Useless*
*Reserved*
*Panic*
*Dejected*
*Desolate*
*Upset*
*Diminished*
*Embarrassed*
*Inferior*
*Weary*

*Nervous*
*Rejected*
*Desperate*
*Bitter*
*Guilty*
*Hesitant*
*Vulnerable*
*Bored*
*Scared*
*Injured*
*Unhappy*
*Aggressive*
*Dissatisfied*
*Shy*
*Empty*
*Preoccupied*
*Worried*
*Offended*
*Lonely*
*Resentful*
*Miserable*
*Disillusioned*
*Forced*
*Cold*
*Frightened*
*Afflicted*
*Mournful*
*Inflamed*
*Disgusting*
*Unbelieving*
*Hesitant*
*Disinterested*
*Timid*

## Feeling Words Chart: Negative

*Aching*
*Dismayed*
*Provoked*
*Terrible*
*Skeptical*
*Despair*
*Lifeless*
*Shaky*
*Victimized*
*Hurt*
*Infuriated*
*In Despair*
*Distrustful*
*Frustrated*
*Numb*
*Restless*
*Heartbroken*
*Weary*
*Cross*
*Sulky*
*Lost*
*Distressed*
*Out of It*
*Doubtful*
*Appalled*
*Broken*
*Worked up*
*A Sense of Loss*
*Unsure*
*Woeful*
*Tired*
*Threatened*
*Humiliated*

*Boiling*
*Flat*
*Pessimistic*
*In a Stew*
*Stuck*
*Quaking*
*Wronged*
*Fuming*
*Tense*
*Dominated*
*Wary*
*Alienated*

# NOTES

www.ingramcontent.com/pod-product-compliance
Lightning Source LLC
Chambersburg PA
CBHW071351290426
44108CB00014B/1505